the

LONNY

home

the LONNY *home*

DISCOVERING & CULTIVATING YOUR MOST AUTHENTIC SPACE

Table of Contents

8 Introduction

Chapter One: Meditating on Your Space

18   Introduction

22   Refined Eclectic: Jenna Barnet & Stephen Butler

30   Lonny Lesson: Four Ways to Address Your Architecture

32   Mood Master: Chris Benz

40   Lonny Lesson: Let There Be Light

44   Earthy Splendor: Lizzie Fortunato & Peter Asbill

50   Two Takes on Meditating on Your Space: Kendra Smoot & Paula Mallis

52   Maine Appeal: Michele Michael and Patrick Moore

60   The Art of the Oasis

62   Miami Zen: Abby Kellet

Chapter Two: Letting It Go—or Making It for Keeps

74   Introduction

78   Minimalist Mission: Karla Gallardo

86   Two Takes on Letting It Go: Wiebke Liu & Caitlin Flemming

88   Gilty Pleasure: Jeet Sohal

96   The Art of the Shelfie

98   Easeful Elegance: Elettra Wiedemann & Caleb Lane

106 Lonny Lesson: Four Ways to Create Functional Storage

108 No-Fuss Chic: Si Mazouz

116 Lonny Lesson: Four Ways to Update Boring Furniture

118 Neon Dreams: Manish Arora

Chapter Three: Seeking Your Inspiration

130 Introduction

132 Bold Restraint: Michael Woodcock & Lara Apponyi

134 Two Takes on Seeking Your Inspiration: Tze Chun & Carly Nance

136 Form Marries Function: Ivy Siosi & Audi Culver

152 Lonny Lesson: Four Ways to Display a Vignette

154 Bohemian Luxury: Christina Bryant

162 Lonny Lesson: Four Ways to Treat Yourself to a Trend

164 Bijou Joy: Cecilia Casagrande

172 The Art of the Table

174 Lush Life: Hilton Carter

Table of Contents

Chapter Four: Putting It All Together

186   Introduction

190   Restorative Classics: Peter Som

198   Two Takes on Putting It All Together:
Jill Singer & Monica Khemsurov & Piera Gelardi

200   Color Theory: Morgan Hutchinson

208   Lonny Lesson: Four Ways to Play with Color

210   Dream Weaver: Aelfie Oudghiri

218   Lonny Lesson: Four Ways to Play with Materials and Texture

220   Grand Designs: Tamara Kaye-Honey

228   The Art of the Floorplan

230   The Bare Essentials: Hrishikesh Hirway & Lindsey Lund Mortensen

Chapter Five: Maintaining Your Truth

242   Introduction

246   Two Takes on Maintaining Your Truth:
      Latham Thomas & Jessica Lanyadoo

248   The A List: Desanka Fasiska

256   Lonny Lesson: Four Ways to Mix Different Styles

258   Cottage Industry: Nic Taylor & Jennifer Brandt-Taylor

266   The Art of the Gallery Wall

268   Room to Grow: Jodie Patterson

276   Lonny Lesson: Four Ways to Introduce Life with Plants

278   A Big Move: Dabito & Ryan

Introduction

Homes are personal. They're where we seek refuge from the constant bustle of the outside world; where we set aside the masks we put on for others and allow ourselves to just be. They are sanctuaries where we nurture our families, build our relationships, and experience our most private moments of joy and grief.

At *Lonny*, we have always felt honored to be invited into people's homes. A lot (and we do mean a lot) of amazing spaces come across our desks every day. But, what is it that really makes a home stand out?

For us, it's authenticity—that feeling that an owner has eschewed all the rules of "good" decorating and instead crafted a space that's uniquely perfect for them. It's looking at a home and knowing that every piece has been mindfully placed and has meaning for the person who lives there. Maybe it's an old relic passed along from family, a flea-market find the person couldn't live without, or an art collection that reflects a life's journey. It all just makes sense. Even if it doesn't.

And after years of curating gorgeous homes online, we wanted to take the next step with this book and help you cultivate spaces that reflect everything you are and everything you hope to be.

SO, HOW SHOULD YOU USE THIS BOOK?

Listen, we don't want to tell you how to decorate. We're here to be your partner and guide you through a journey of discovering what truly matters to you – in your home and in your life. We've laid out this path to cultivating your most authentic home with these guideposts in mind:

Reflect   Let go   Explore   Activate   Evolve

(and then repeat as often as you like)

Every chapter will feature memorable *Lonny* homes that really showcase the ethos of each chapter. We've also sought out advice from inspirational figures who offer refreshing perspectives on maintaining personal creativity in a world fueled by changing trends and commercialism. And every chapter also has some nitty-gritty practical advice you can immediately apply to your home.

We hope that at the end of this book, you can take a deep breath and approach your home with fresh eyes. Maybe even find new meaning and consideration for your belongings, layout, or even the problem areas your home may have. We hope to help you learn to truly love your space and cultivate the kind of energy that is important to you. Because we are all on a path, and our homes should reflect our journeys. So let's get started on making your home your haven.

xo
Angela Tafoya, Editorial Director
Jill Slattery, Chief Content Officer

CHAPTER ONE

Meditating on Your Space

If the current vogue for wellness is any indication, our lives could all use a little more R&R: reflection and relaxation. With so much "noise" infiltrating our spaces—from headspace to living space—it makes sense that our interior lives, like our interiors themselves, are in need of some rearranging.

*A*nd we don't mean just scooting a vase to the left or hanging a print a bit lower—we mean initiating a fundamental shift in energies and acknowledging the ways they affect us. To that end, this chapter is all about exploring your home as an extension of your mind space.

It's no news that architecture and interior design influence our mood—we didn't end up with feng shui and a whole industry dedicated to color forecasting without first having a hunch that aesthetics can impact our psyches. Neuroscience has chimed in too, demonstrating, for instance, that rooms with high ceilings lead to greater creativity, increasing our capacity for abstract thought, while more constrained spaces might be best for tasks that require intense focus, according to a study at the Carlson School of Management. We even know that the hippocampus—that teeny part of the brain that governs long- and short-term memory, as well as navigation—is uniquely attuned to the symmetry and flow in the spaces we call home.

Another thing we've learned from science? Stress is bad for us. For this reason, you should make every effort to ensure that your home is a reprieve from the things that stress you out, whether that's the news cycle or the challenge of managing your own time. It can help to remember that our homes also have to work for us—think of them as well-oiled machines that help us stay organized and ready for the day. With information moving at the speed of light, it's more important than ever to set boundaries and clarify what you need and want from your environment. Meditating on your space is how you'll get there. (Don't worry, there's no chanting involved!)

Meditating on your space means nothing less than asking yourself who you are and how you want to live. Our goal is to help you embrace your inspirations and harness your passions to create an oasis that feels personal and authentic. Meditation in this sense isn't a passive act of escapism, but an empowering act of intention. Here are a few things to keep in mind when you decide to sit down and do it.

ASK YOURSELF CLARIFYING QUESTIONS

Your home should be a space that facilitates action—that supports you in all the things you do there. You don't need to be a professional organizer or an interior designer to investigate how each of your rooms can help you lead a smarter, healthier life. Try first identifying the pain points in your daily routine. If you feel distress getting out of the house every morning, take a look at the role your space plays in that anxiety—you may have a chaotic closet or disordered entryway working against you. Or perhaps you rarely make a meal even though you like cooking; a straight-up joyless kitchen may be the culprit. Then flip the question around: Which spaces in your home make life more pleasurable? Which make you tackle tasks with vigor? Which do you enjoy sharing with others? Take a moment to linger in those spots and identify their root magic.

ENVISION NEW POSSIBILITIES

Since your home is an extension of yourself, it's important to make time to investigate its potential. Pause for a moment and—in your mind's eye—move everything out, taking your home back to the blank slate it was when you first moved in. Then visualize the life you want to lead there. See yourself waking up and going through the day in those rooms, and think about how those empty spaces could be configured to make life sweeter. Don't worry about Pinterest or money or whether you keep your grandmother's armoire. Just daydream, letting your mind fill your home with the people and memories, activities and hobbies, furnishings and art, and textures and colors that it craves. Whatever you see, make a quick sketch or take a few notes.

SET INTENTIONS FOR YOUR SPACE

Now that you've figured out which areas are (and aren't!) helping you live your best life, it's time to declare some goals, or—in wellness speak—set your intentions. This doesn't necessarily mean drafting a to-do list of home-improvement projects or making resolutions that will help you actualize the ideal space you just envisioned, though it can. In truth, setting your intentions can take many different forms. For Paula Mallis, whom we profile on page 51, it meant defining possibility, making a conscious choice to let certain energies in and to keep others out. She then created a space that reflects and upholds those values— from the materials she chose to the personal and professional boundaries she identified and now enforces. But for others, setting intention might be as simple as saying, "This is where the desk goes because this view will brighten my day." Just remain open to feedback, from the universe or otherwise.

In short, your home needs to fortify you in your ambitions, providing the space you need in order to grow, build, and learn—as well as the ability to pass those lessons along. We do this by cultivating a sense of self, harnessing the emotional power of the possessions that inspire us and channeling our desires into the spaces that we shape. Over the course of this chapter, we'll look at easy and effective ways to solve for zen-zapping problem areas (rental lighting, be gone!) and real stories from home and business owners who've made their intentions manifest through trial and error and— you guessed it—meditating on their spaces.

Refined Eclectic

"My intention was to create a loving place for the family," says designer Kim Gordon about the light-filled home she helped Jenna Barnet and Stephen Butler to manifest in Venice, California. Their space is a perfect example of how to set and follow through on your best intentions. "Our home is the epicenter of our universe," says Barnet. "It is the place we never want to leave, and it is perfectly attuned to who we are as people and as a family."

The idea of being in harmony with our surroundings shouldn't be reserved for spa trips or nature walks—after all, the number-one space we retreat to is home. For Barnet and Butler, who live near the beach, a relaxed lifestyle isn't hard to come by. "Venice is one of the most amazing places on the planet. It is a creative, surfy, and community-driven center filled with energy and ideas," says Barnet.

Working with designer Gordon, the couple used unique handmade elements for a personal touch, injecting liveliness into the home's many quiet corners. Barnet chose all the art herself, including some pieces made by her husband. "I am without a doubt a minimalist, while Stephen prefers layers," she says. "We have a constant and healthy tension—I want less and he wants more—[but] I have learned so much

from Stephen's aesthetic and artistic sensibilities." Many of these pieces found a place in the library, the hub of the home. "Stephen and I spend most evenings unwinding there, looking through books and talking about the day over a glass of wine."

For creative types like Barnet and Butler, the notion of transparency—in both the physical and the emotional senses—is the key to a happy home. Their space reflects an intentional openness and stripped-down approach that helps showcase the curios that the family has carefully collected as well as the life that they lead there.

Ever intentional, this family chose floor-to-ceiling windows to foster a sense of emotional transparency.

According to Barnet, it all starts with the floor-to-ceiling windows. "They were made for the house and bring in so much light and richness, giving it an incredible artisanal quality," she notes. You can also see this idea at work in their open kitchen, which is wrapped with glass shelves that allow for free exchange between those cooking and those enjoying the main living area.

These elements have a sense of light and reflection, Barnet adds, "characteristics that add to the openness of the environment." The final result is a sort of lived-in museum, beautifully curated yet warm and real.

PREVIOUS SPREAD / STAYING GROUNDED

The raw-oak floors are some of Barnet's favorite features. She says they give uniformity to the house. Barnet bought the velvet sectional on eBay and the coral side chairs from HD Buttercup. "This house was a dream to furnish—it holds things so well," Barnet says. "We wanted our furniture to feel unique, but also reflect a refined but utilitarian sensibility."

OPPOSITE / EMBEDDING SURPRISES

The kitchen surprises with colorful tile bedecking the floor, a chandelier towering above the stove,

and—of course—the glass shelving that amplifies the natural light in the space. Spaced as if on display in a museum, the vases appear to float.

ABOVE, LEFT / COLOR WITH INTENTION

Throughout the home, blue tones add a calm and serene vibe and a sense of collected cool, while pops of bright yellow lend liveliness.

ABOVE, RIGHT / MINDING THE DETAILS

Barnet and Butler's impressive library is peppered with art pieces. The sculpture resting on the ladder was made by Barnet himself.

ABOVE / A LANDING PAD WORTH LINGERING ON

Touches of personality can be seen throughout the home—like the stylish seating area on the landing and the pictures casually but deliberately leaned against the wall. (This is a great way to keep a gallery of rotating artwork, and photos on the floor and along the window also lead the eye all over the room, too, creating visual interest.)

OPPOSITE / SOAKING IT ALL IN

If any room in the house should be configured for meditative moments, it's the master bath—and this light-flooded and pared-back oasis definitely fits the bill. The bathroom has the only shielded windows in the house. Barnet notes that Stephen is from Dutch ancestry, a culture in which "Everything inside is considered outside and vice versa."

It's crucial that every home have its zen den—a space where you can get away from it all and reconnect with what matters.

Four Ways to Address Your Architecture

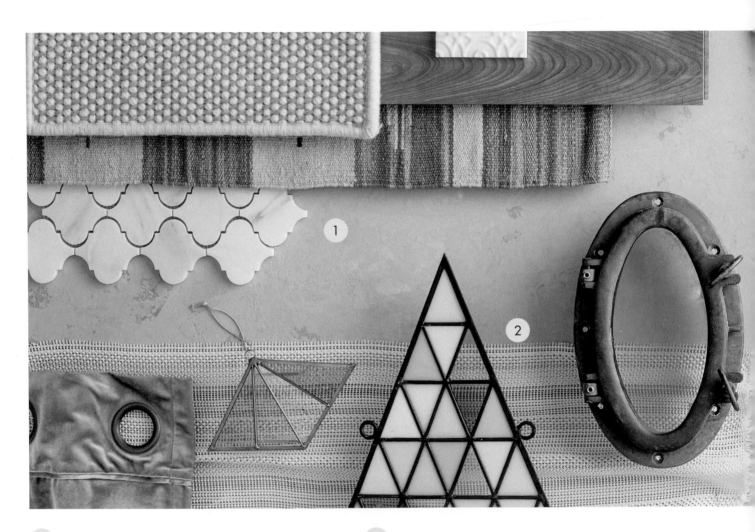

1 BUILD FROM THE GROUND UP

From dated carpet to scratched hardwood, ugly floors can be a huge headache. If you have hardwood floors, look at the wood grain and tone and decide if they're worth showing off, or if they might be better covered with an area rug or wall-to-wall carpet. For a bold choice, consider painting wooden floors—but be sure you do your research. Laminate or vinyl flooring and tiles likely won't take paint well. For new materials, bamboo is a relatively eco-friendly material that's also easy to maintain.

2 DRESS YOUR WINDOWS

Window coverings may be a standard fitting, but that doesn't mean they can't be a focal point. Shades come in a variety of styles, fabrics, and colors, and blinds can bring in elements of wood, aluminum, or vinyl. Floor-length drapery can be used to create a sense of height and drama, and shorter styles will have the same benefits of alternately blocking the sun and framing your view. You can also try frosted or otherwise treated glass to set a mood.

In the process of meditating on your space, you'll be taking a deep look around—and that may highlight some things you plain don't like about it. Fear not: While a home's bones and materials may seem unchangeable without great expense, you can do a lot with simple switches, cover-ups, and additions to mask problem areas and boost character.

3 WITH ALL THE TRIMMINGS, PLEASE

Trimming your space can feel superfluous or fussy, but when done right, those little touches can make all the difference between a home that feels pulled together and a home that feels . . . less so. Wooden accents like decorative wainscoting, crown moldings, window frames, and ceiling medallions look great stained or painted to feel like a piece of the original property. These tricks can even create a sense of history within a space that would otherwise feel more modern.

4 SWEAT THE SMALL STUFF

You don't have to rip out your kitchen cabinets just because they're fugly. You can give them an all-new (almost) look by upgrading the hardware, swapping outdated handles and knobs for fresher styles. This approach works throughout the house, with faucets, door handles, and locks, coordinating new ones with what's existing—and permanent. Cohesion looks expensive. Being mindful of small details like wall hooks in the entryway can also make a big difference overall.

Mood Master

Although the word *meditation* starts with *me*, considering your space with intention needn't result in a complete undoing of the design choices of those who came before you. In fact, the outcome can be even dreamier when you build up instead of tear down. Case in point: the story of creative director Chris Benz, whose space reflects his personality yet respects the home's past. Benz purchased his historic 1905 Brooklyn brownstone in 2014; over three years, he designed a dynamic, hue-saturated home that feels modern and intriguing, steeped in history but not bogged down by tradition. "I grew up spending lots of time at my grandparents' house in Port Madison, Bainbridge Island," says Benz. "It was this terrific red ship-captain's house from 1850. That love of old houses and decorating has never escaped me."

Starting with a binder full of inspiration, a lengthy renovation paved the way to what is now Benz's dream home. Key to that sweet smell of success? "I had a plan months before closing, so I was as prepared as possible," says Benz. "My approach—since I intended to live on-site while working on the property—was to work from the top floor, finish, and move down. In retrospect, it really made no difference, cleanliness-wise, because no amount of taping-off rooms prevents dust and debris from going everywhere!"

The house itself had remained remarkably untouched, lived in by only one family since it was built at the turn of the 20th century. Benz retained as much of the original detailing

We love a home that honors history while leaning into the present. Benz took his time to get the details just right.

as possible, using salvaged and period-specific materials where refinishing felt necessary. "It was integral to me to re-establish the house in as close to its original layout and form as possible. With this house in particular, [it was hard] to find period-appropriate fixtures and hardware that felt modern and unfussy without being too expensive. I wanted to breathe life back into a great house that had really fallen into disrepair, but I did not want it to feel like a museum."

The kitchen and mudroom were the biggest projects, as Benz approached each of those rooms as a blank slate. Everything was custom-made for the space—only the floors are original. "The ceiling was collapsing, and there were a couple of old cabinets to remove," remembers Benz. Now, guests congregate around the kitchen island to pour themselves drinks from the built-in wet bar or whip up meals on the Bertazzoni range.

Less of a challenge was color. For Benz, color at home is all about creating livable palettes. "For example," he says "I rarely use more than one color per room. It's better to create a rich background and spice it up with furniture and smaller pieces." Using Farrow & Ball paints throughout, Benz created a space that is at once moody and utterly livable, expertly straddling the line between precious and pragmatic. "It was so important to come up with a formula for each room—floor sanding, skim-coating, paint—so that there were fewer variables. I guess it's all my experience working with factories overseas: set up the system, approve it, and flush it through."

For now, Benz says that the house is complete. But there is always more to do, and always ways to perfect—millwork, built-ins, and moldings, oh my! "But my Parsons' education necessitates knowing when to stop," says Benz. "And to always leave something unfinished."

PREVIOUS SPREAD / SETTING THE SCENE
FOR CONTEMPLATION
The back parlor features a vintage Swedish floating globe fixture,
vintage Milo Baughman lounge chairs in the original tie-dye mohair
velvet(!), and—at the center—a striking sculpture by Ernest Trova.
Benz tried to preserve as much of the home as he could and the tile
around the fireplace was one of the features he kept.

OPPOSITE / A CREATIVE NOOK
Chris Benz at home at his desk. The creative director for fashion
house Bill Blass has tons of inspiration pinned up in his work space.

ABOVE, LEFT & RIGHT / CURIOUS FLASHES
There's endless inspiration in Benz's office—including this vintage
matador jacket and Japanese screen.

Color seriously impacts your home's happiness quotient. Benz's progression from romantic pastels to deep and moody blues is everything.

OPPOSITE TOP & BOTTOM / LOVELY LIMITED PALETTES

For creating a room doused with color that's still approachable, Benz typically sticks to one hue. "I love mixing color and texture, and that extends to decorating as well," he explains. "For home, though, it's really about creating balanced, livable palettes that are unobtrusive." A honey-yellow wall color in the guest bedroom furthers the sense of homespun welcome, while a distinctly modern plant choice—the pencil cactus provides a little edge.

LEFT / THINKING PINK

A religious portrait on glass hangs above a Restoration Hardware bed, a Steiff mohair throw, a Comme des Garçons afghan, and Target—yes, Target!—sheets. When asked how he wants guests to feel when they enter his home, Benz replies "Welcomed and comfortable. I always want my home to feel like your favorite bed and breakfast."

FOLLOWING PAGE / THE OMBRE OPTION

When it came to paint, Benz planned for the house to follow a gradient (with the hallways, stairs, and ground floor neutral). The back parlor is painted in an inky dark blue while in the front sitting room Benz used an invigorating cerulean.

Four Ways to Let There Be Light

1 SET THE MOOD WITH AMBIENT LIGHT

Ambient lighting is the first main category of illumination, and it includes the natural light a room receives as well as more permanent installed fixtures (often overhead), like recessed lighting, pendants, chandeliers, and ceiling lights. These are the main sources of light and are often quite bright, so it's important to be sensitive to how they can affect your mood. Some tasks or gatherings benefit from bold illumination, but be mindful when "mood lighting" means less, not more.

2 ILLUMINATE ZONES WITH SMALL LIGHTS

There are two types of zone lighting: Task lighting is dedicated to specific areas and actions within a room, such as a reading lamp, while accent lighting is usually decorative—adding ambiance without overwhelming wattage. Floor and table lamps enhance small spaces, define areas within a room, and call attention to points of interest. When overhead lighting is too harsh for a gathering, such as a dinner party, dim accent lights and candles give a welcome glow.

We're huge fans of natural light and will always encourage solutions that maximize the sunshine. Still, there's more to staging a well-lit room than simply pulling open the blinds. Whether your goal is to entertain year-round or craft the perfect relaxation nook, here's how to approach lighting so that all your spaces are beautifully lit.

3 BOUNCE LIGHT WITH REFLECTION

Mirrors can add depth and dimension, amplifying great artworks or simply reflecting light where it might not otherwise reach. Placed strategically, they can make a room appear larger, especially when used to scale. But you don't have to go full floor-to-ceiling with your mirrors to get a taste of their benefits: Small decorative objects that are mirrored or made of glass or other translucent materials will also reflect light around a smaller space for a similar effect.

4 KEEP IT BRIGHT WITH WHITE

Since they also bounce light, white walls, floors, and surfaces make a big difference in a room's light level. They also have a tried-and-true effect on your perception of a space. Whites with warm undertones are great for making main living areas feel open yet energetic, while bedrooms get a calming effect from cooler undertones—the perfect way to ease into sleep. Sheer white textiles can diffuse light, too, making for a softer illumination. If white feels too stark, try pale blues.

Earthy Splendor

Jewelry designer Lizzie Fortunato's Brooklyn home is #goals incarnate: an historic brownstone with oodles of charm where she and her husband, Peter Asbill, like to spend their weekends listening to bluegrass and making waffles. The couple has created a space that vibrates with good energy and simple sophistication. It's a fitting setting for Fortunato, whose jewelry designs are by turns contemplative and abstract—a nod to the past couched in modern materials.

Her home reflects that same sensibility, with its reverence for '70s glam infused with touches of the jet set, but down-to-earth and fittingly homespun. In a word: Brooklyn. Which is why it's so surprising to find that she was a staunch Manhattanite until just a few short years ago. After living with her twin sister, Kathryn, in a minuscule Soho gem friends dubbed "the doll house," friend Taylor Patterson of floral design studio Fox Fodder Farm moved to Clinton Hill and began extolling the neighborhood's virtues. Fortunato considered making the move herself and began trolling listings online; she thought this space was too good to be true and contacted the rental agent in the wee hours of the morning. The next day, she signed a contract.

The sisters initially made the move together, though today the space is shared by Lizzie

and Peter. The couple's nest is filled with earthy textiles and bold colors, as well as moments of reprieve. "I'm so attracted to the way textiles reflect specific geographies," says Fortunato, who often brings them back from her travels to locations such as Morocco and Turkey. "This apartment has provided the best backdrop (and most space) for the things that I love," she says. "[But] I don't think I'm ever going to be like, OK, this is how it's going to be for the next ten years." Her philosophy? Don't worry about the little things, and don't rush major purchases. "It's scary to feel like you can't change it again."

It didn't help the home's zen quotient that, for a period, Fortunato was using it to store all of the inventory for Fortune Finds—a collection of found pieces and curios from her travels that she sells online. To give the collection space and highlight key pieces, Fortunato is given to lots of rearranging and mixing, constantly teasing and tweaking the layouts and arrangements on tables, shelves, and trays. This is partly due to a lack of storage, which necessitates a keen eye for accommodating assemblages, but it also comes from the quiet confidence of asserting a point of view as a brand. "Minimalism is never going to be for me," she says. During the early years of the line, Fortunato used to go out of her way to keep the office neat and tidy. Pinterest added to the existential pressure to keep up appearances, but in the end she concedes, "A mess means we're successful." Now, she moderates her buying impulses out of necessity and finds plenty of time to relax and center herself in her space. "I feel so 'on' at the office, I definitely want my home to be a sanctuary." So, you *can* take the girl out of Manhattan—just make sure to bring the waffles.

Envisioning possibilities for your home is an ongoing practice—Lizzie does it right by hitting refresh whenever the whim strikes.

PREVIOUS PAGE / A WELCOMING HUB

Lizzie Fortunato and Peter Asbill's Clinton Hill townhouse qualifies as a dream city apartment—starting with their dining room. Above the fireplace, a painting by artist and friend Sally King Benedict overlooks the dining room, where the couple loves to entertain.

OPPOSITE / STEPPING OUT

Lizzie and husband Peter Asbill proudly stand on the stoop of their Clinton Hill abode. Once a sworn Manhattanite, Fortunato made the move to this Brooklyn spot with her sister before Asbill moved in.

ABOVE LEFT / HONING IN ON THE DETAILS

A close-up detail of a tasseled wall hanging from Manhattan store Adaptations, which makes for a statement piece in the dining room. While the piece's overall tone is natural, small pops of brightly colored thread wrapped around each tassel give it a decidedly modern feel.

ABOVE RIGHT / GOING CUSTOM

"I was on the most endless hunt for a sideboard that felt simple, modern, and sophisticated," says Lizzie. This custom-made credenza from Daniel Morrison of Yucca Stuff is one of her favorite pieces.

OPPOSITE / BAR'S OPEN

"Peter was adamant about having a good bar in the kitchen," says Lizzie. Forgoing the trendy, gilded bar cart look, the couple settled on a vintage medicine cart to serve up Aperol spritzes and tequila negronis.

ABOVE / MIXING IN TRAVEL FINDS

An 80-year-old Turkish carpet that Lizzie's sister Kathryn brought back from the Grand Bazaar in Istanbul hangs on the wall of the open living and kitchen area. It's hung over a rack for a more casual feel, and plays well with travel-inspired motifs and the warm tones of the throw pillows and rugs.

OPPOSITE / MORE THAN A BENCH

This beautiful custom bench lends the dining room an unexpected shape and offers a landing pad for nicely stacked books and a sparse arrangement of decorative objects, letting the tapestry overhead take center stage.

ABOVE / GETTING LOW

Upstairs, gleaming wide-plank wood floors stretch across a low-key living area. Fortunato has placed decorative objects—a birdcage, an oversize vase, and a cleverly repurposed wooden trough—directly on the floor for a intriguing undone look.

Don't be afraid of negative space. It lets prized possessions sing, and gives your eye—and mind—a bit of a break.

Two Takes on Meditating on Your Space

ADVICE FROM KENDRA SMOOT, STYLIST

Stylist and Bay Area transplant Kendra Smoot is no stranger to a beautiful image. "We joke that Instagram made us move to California," she says with a laugh. It's not that she and her husband, Seth, decided to take their brood across country for the sake of the 'gram—though that Golden State light is admittedly hard to beat. It's a lifestyle change that the industry insider notes has benefited her personal and creative growth. And it's an energy that's reflected at home.

SETTING BOUNDARIES

"There was a time when I was putting the kids to bed and then working for five hours," remembers Smoot. Now, the working mother keeps strict boundaries between her professional and private lives by keeping to a more regular schedule, storing props outside the home, and using tools like Pinterest to corral inspiration instead of letting it overtake her walls.

CLARIFYING INTENTIONS

The Smoots didn't undertake any major renovations aside from removing one wall to create a more loft-like space. One added benefit is that it facilitates conversation and connection. "The lighting in our place is low, like mood lighting," notes Smoot, who says that the zen quality of the interior has created natural "hang zones" throughout. "I love to have people over; [entertaining] really makes you think about what are those things in a space that make you really want to be there—smells like palo santo and essential oils, and having a fire going."

FOCUS ON MATERIALS

Fittingly, the Smoots' home is midcentury in style, with "cabin-y" vibes. "We have a lot of wood and natural elements that we live in sync with," says Smoot. They also went to town with white paint as a kind of baptism. "All the colors I use [in my work] are really calm, and now I want to evolve my aesthetic and grow it—less with color and more with texture." Her family home is a studied reflection of that. (And, yes, her Instagram still speaks to it, too.)

ADVICE FROM PAULA MALLIS, MEDITATION GURU

When it comes to bringing good energy home, Paula Mallis's reputation precedes her. The doula and spiritual counselor isn't a professional organizer, nor is she an interior decorator. It was having her first child—or, as Mallis also refers to it, transitioning from maiden to mother—that pushed her to separate her home life from her work life, creating WMN Space (a women-only meditation and movement retreat in Los Angeles) in the process.

SETTING BOUNDARIES

Mallis originally started holding space for women in her own home, but those sessions quickly grew in size, presenting a real problem for the family. "We decided we had to put building a home first, but the feedback we always got about our space was that people walked in and felt at ease." The couple brought that same energy to WMN Space. "By the time [clients] have walked to the top of the stairs they're just like, 'Oh, yes, I'm so glad I showed up here today!' " Mallis says with a laugh.

CLARIFYING INTENTIONS

Mallis set her intentions for the space, which she knew would need to facilitate both meditative and active energies, depending on a client's needs. She made a point to rid herself and her surroundings of negative energy as well as clutter. "Every time you declutter, you're dumping the unconscious," says Mallis. (We'll talk more about this in chapter 2!)

FOCUS ON MATERIALS

Mallis and her husband, Todd, a designer and builder, had numerous conversations about their space and how it could articulate their shared principles through design. An expanse of white oak beneath visitors' feet has a grounding effect—there are no shoes allowed—"so immediately when you walk in you feel connected to the earth," notes Mallis. Plants are important for their similarly earthy effect ("They thrive in the space"), while natural materials and textures continue throughout to reaffirm a connectedness to something larger than the self.

Maine Appeal

Floor-to-ceiling windows and an open floor plan make for a modern-treehouse effect at the home of ceramist Michele Michael and woodworker Patrick Moore. Located in the remote Maine town of Dresden, about an hour away from Portland, the three-story home—surrounded by forest and looking out onto the Eastern River—provides an intimate view of the local wildlife: eagles, owls, herons, turkeys, foxes, and beavers, to name just a few.

In 2002, after vacationing on the coast, the Brooklyn, New York, couple purchased the three-bedroom house as a second home. That refuge from the breakneck pace of city life proved too alluring to pass up, and so in 2014, they decided to sell their apartment and make a permanent move. "I had a wonderful career in New York, but once I fell in love with working with clay, I knew it would give me the opportunity to live in Maine full-time," says Michael, a former prop stylist and magazine editor, whose line, Elephant Ceramics, celebrates painterly washes of color and handmade textures. "We had long dreamed

of moving to the country, and my ceramics helped make it happen." In Maine, envisioning the possibilities of their new home was all about creating a full-time haven for the couple's creative priorities—Michael's ceramics and Moore's woodworking—as well as putting them in close and constant contact with a huge source of their work's inspiration: nature.

After a flurry of home-improvement projects, which included replacing the chimney, insulating the basement, and putting in stone walkways— "not very glamorous, but necessary," Michael admits—the couple turned their attention to the interiors. Moore's clean-lined custom furnishings mix easily with midcentury classics, Moroccan textiles, and a varied array of artworks (many from the couple's own friends), while Michael's dominant palette of blues and creams provides a cohesive motif and a connection to that original source of tranquility and inspiration: the great outdoors. "The earthy, watery quality of my glazing and textures comes directly from the beautiful little tidal pools, seaweed beds, lichen-covered granite, and ocean waves," she says.

The biggest project was the barn, which was built from the ground up and now serves as both a ceramics studio and a woodworking shop. Here, color is carefully considered: White walls allow chosen surfaces, such as a work table built by Moore to stand out in shades of blue. (Even the North Star slab roller was chosen for its eye-catching hue.)

Michael's advice for cultivating a space that feels fresh and considered? Keep it moving, never static. She frequently rearranges her furnishings, artwork, and accessories, editing along the way. "I suppose this is a hazard of being a prop stylist for so many years!"

Your home should help you do what you love. This dreamy retreat is all about creative sanctuary.

PREVIOUS PAGE /
HIGHLIGHTING THE BEAUTY OF WOOD
Many of the home's interiors showcase wood in its close-to-natural state, including this sunny corner of the living room with a Danish teak console and an Eames lounge chair, upholstered in dark blue leather.

OPPOSITE / BLUE STREAK
Michael's recent firings rest in her studio. "When I unload the kiln, I usually cover the table and sit with those pieces for a little while," she says. "I chose a palette of signature blues for my glazes because food, for the most part, looks beautiful on blue."

ABOVE LEFT / TEAM EFFORT
Michele Michael and Patrick Moore in front of the barn they built at their home. To create it, the couple hosted an all-day barn raising, with many friends stopping by to help. "I'm very thankful for the community we live in," Michael says. The structure has an oak-and-pine frame, built with trees from the surrounding forest.

ABOVE RIGHT / MERGING RUSTIC WITH MODERN
In the dining room, the Cross Cable light fixture by David Weeks adds contemporary edge to the rural scene, while echoing the shape of the stag horns in the painting by Jared DeFrancesco. While big fans of natural wood, a few major pieces in their home also feature painted surfaces, including the blue-top Shaker-style dining table built by Moore.

OPPOSITE / WATER WORLD
The color choices in Michael and Moore's home
reflect their beautiful views of the Eastern River.

ABOVE / SHOWING OFF
A SATURATED SHADE
Inspired by a room at the Paul Smith boutique in
Manhattan, Michael chose a turquoise wall paint
for the master bedroom and a similarly hued cotton
coverlet from Morocco. She then added subtlety
with complementary colors, such as a brown leather
bedside chair and burgundy wildflowers.

*Lonny challenge alert!
Re-create a palette from
nature for a room that's both
ethereal and grounding.*

ABOVE, LEFT / PUTTING IT ALL OUT THERE
In the kitchen, Moore designed and built the open shelving to hold his wife's collection of vintage cocktail glasses and handmade ceramics. The Prussian-blue cabinetry was inspired by a visit to the Sabbathday Lake Shaker Village in New Gloucester, Maine, where blue milk paint was used for the flooring and wall paneling in several buildings.

ABOVE, RIGHT / STUDIO DAYS
Michael at work in her barn studio, with her cobalt-blue North Star slab roller to her left and pieces from her collection lining the shelves and table behind her.

OPPOSITE / A MEANINGFUL COLLECTION
Much of the couple's art was amassed through exchanges with other artists. Given the wide-ranging mix of styles, Michael embraces the eclecticism: "I feel strongly that if you have a group of objects you love, they will somehow all work together."

THE ART OF THE OASIS

Scent can be a powerful tool in meditation—plus, it really makes a difference in a space. Aromatherapy can help you bring a little bit of serenity into your own home, giving you the time to reflect on how you're living and why. It's also an empowering way to manifest your priorities. Here are some of our favorite techniques for achieving peak peace through scent.

POTPOURRI Dry a potent mix of flowers and collect them in a bowl or sachet. To increase their effect, add a few drops of your preferred essential oil and bake them in the oven to infuse them with the fragrance. Scent is served!

ESSENTIAL OILS An ancient way to bring peace into your home, citrus scents like lemon or orange can have an uplifting effect on your mood, encouraging creativity and positive thinking. Yes, please!

CANDLES An accessible and powerful tool for creating dynamic olfactory experiences, candles are also easy on the eyes—and tea-light jars can be repurposed! They come in a variety of scents and intensities and can be layered over one another if you burn two at a time.

SAGE & PALO SANTO Burn sage to cleanse your aura and benefit from its healing properties, or light up palo santo—both practices have been performed by native and indigenous cultures for centuries—to help keep you grounded, connected, and ready to take on the world. Both keep bad energy at bay and can evoke powerful scent memories.

INCENSE
Burning incense sticks or cones can inspire clarity and peace of mind, with a scent redolent of tradition.

Miami Zen

Abby Kellett's pastel-drenched Miami family home deftly melds bold tropical influences with the clean, sophisticated lines of Nordic living. "I wanted to combine the two," says Kellett. "Every room has a major element of color, but the overall feeling is still quite calm and minimal." It's a rarefied balance that wasn't easy to come by. "The house was a little crazy when we bought it," admits Kellett. "It had glittery popcorn ceilings and a carpeted, raised-concrete platform in the living room, but I loved the layout and the Spanish-style exterior. At the time, I was the only one who could see its potential."

Now, the space reflects Kellett's varied interests and tastes as the proprietor of online emporium Gretel Home. "For me, each room or vignette needs to have a variety of textures and materials—nothing too matchy," says Kellett. "A mixture of ceramics, glass, metal, fabrics, leather, paper, and paint, new and vintage, and always something natural like flowers, a table made from a tree trunk, or a wild-looking branch." In the dining room, London-based artist Marthe Armitage's Chestnut wallpaper adorns the walls, a decorative splurge years in the making. "I just knew that I wanted [that paper] in charcoal gray and sent her a paint swatch," says Kellett. "I'm sure it will always be my favorite thing in the house."

The home's outdoor terrace is one of its best design features, allowing the family to make the most of one of the best things about living in Miami. "I love the weather and not having to think about what to wear in the mornings," says Kellett. "My husband uses [the outdoor shower] every day of the year—no matter how cold it gets!" She adds that the keys to a happy home are truly "family and AC."

Another major factor in this home's oasis appeal? Its wonderful palette, which pairs earthy hues with graphic stripes in pastel pink and blue. The overall effect is both grounding

Don't be deterred by those who don't get your home's potential. It's your space— let your vision guide you.

and uplifting, connecting the home to the beach's driftwood and sand, pristine waters, and rose-streaked sunsets. "The pink of [daughter] Beatrice's room is peachy," Kellett says. "It's pink but not too girly and acts almost as a neutral. It works with pretty much any other color."

Kellett's interpretation of Scandi style likely has real wellness benefits as well. The Danes are consistently rated among the world's happiest people, an accomplishment that researchers have correlated to their low-stress approach to spending quality time at home. Kellett's Miami minimalist abode definitely qualifies—think of it as hygge for the tropics.

PREVIOUS SPREAD /
HARMONIZING MATERIALS
Kellett's kitchen features a beautifully
synchronized mix of warm, rosy
wood cabinetry and tile in burgundy,
light pink, fawn, and greige.

OPPOSITE LEFT / A BELOVED
SPLURGE
Kellett's beloved Marthe Armitage
wallpaper is hand-printed by the
artist herself (who is in her mid-80s)
in a studio overlooking the River
Thames in London.

OPPOSITE RIGHT / FINDING
PEACE POOLSIDE
Homeowner Abby Kellett cools off in
the Miami heat by the pool.

THIS PAGE / FEELING BLUE
The dining room is the perfect
example of Kellett's love for modern
sensibility and colorful accents.
Above the Xpand table are two
framed Claudia Uribe Touri pieces,
complemented by blue Herman Miller
chairs and a Normann Copenhagen
light fixture. "I already owned the
blue chairs and, as blue and pink is
my favorite color combo, I painted
the pink stripe as their backdrop."

OPPOSITE TOP / GOING WALL TO WALL

Kellett's dreamy kitchen features a single wooden shelf that stretches the length of one wall, where she displays a well-curated collection of ceramics in pastels and crisp white.

OPPOSITE BOTTOM / DREAM PATIO

"I love everything printed in colorful, beautiful pattern," Kellett shares. "Marimekko and Liberty are classic favorites of mine." The wall tile on the patio shows her love of motif: It nods to the home's Spanish origins, now updated with a decidedly modern, constrained, yet fresh colorway.

ABOVE / PAIRING AIRY WITH COZY

Done up in Kellett's signature palette of natural browns and cotton-candy pinks and blues, the living room is grounding—with inviting wool chairs and a deep, low leather sofa anchoring the space—while still being open and light, thanks to a glass Eric Trine coffee table and open shelving.

ABOVE / CRAFTING A SERENE RETREAT

"My approach to styling and decorating is similar and mainly relates to variety," Kellett says. The master bath is a testament to that philosophy. Just beyond the door is an outdoor shower, which is also among Kellett's favorite features of the home. Meanwhile, the master bath's white marble countertops and discreet open storage blend into the tiled walls, and the aqua floor tiles immediately make you feel like you're walking into the sea.

OPPOSITE / A WASHI OF COLOR

Kellett's daughter Beatrice's room features a white IKEA dresser reinvented with Anthropologie knobs. Kellett's DIY skills are pretty impressive—she created the artwork behind the items out of washi tape. "Washi tape is so versatile," she says, noting that it's "forgiving and comes in a multitude of colors. I use it for everything from gift wrapping to covering notebooks."

Kids need spaces to chill too. Try bringing in a child's fave color—like pink—in an intentionally serene way.

CHAPTER TWO

Letting It Go— or Making It for Keeps

Stuff—we've all got it. And while at times the world seems staunchly divided between minimalism fetishists and maximalist crusaders, the method by which you decide what gets pride of place in your home and what gets let go is entirely up to you. It's also not for the faint of heart, so we brought tips.

*I*n our hyperconnected age, it can be hard to separate needs from wants. You've got Alexa looking over your shoulder, suggesting a new brand of paper towels, and a button on your counter that auto-delivers dish soap. Mindfulness means being aware of how all this stuff comes into your home as well as how it will likely leave—what percentage of the things that arrive each day are destined for the bin? For obsolescence?

And our possessions aren't just something we're forced to deal with physically. Objects store energy, and they keep that energy in our homes in very specific ways. As the way we live has shifted, the burden of making our homes look good has fallen onto us mere mortals, armed with Pinterest accounts while still saddled with reality. What we need from our homes has shifted, too, along with the roles we play, the dreams we share, and the number of robots helping out with our domestic duties. Not all of us have space, and not all of us can afford a helping hand to bring our dream home—whether bohemian luxe, erratic aristocratic, or mindfully minimal—to life.

Which brings us to one of the biggest hurdles for homeowners and renters alike: living with stuff. We feel compelled to hold on to things for so many different reasons, and not all of them make sense. You can form a sentimental attachment to a photograph, an old dish towel, or a collection of Beanie Babies. As we age, our relationships with all of those things change, endowing them with memories and finding both new meanings and untapped potential in the old. Deciding what makes your home feel authentically you is a complicated process that involves determining for yourself (and your family) which objects stay and which go. How do they speak to each other and add to a sense of well-being and completeness?

So it's time. Close your eyes, open them again, and look at your home. Prepare to take it back from the objects it houses and return it to the people who live there.

QUESTION YOUR POSSESSIONS

Ask these questions of the stuff in your life: Do I use it once a month or more? Is it good quality? Do I have it in multiples? Not everything needs to have a function, but it shouldn't get in the way of your functioning. If you're being attacked by stacks of plates every time you put the dishes away, then, Houston, we have a problem. Also pause to think of these objects as conduits for experience: What kinds of moments do they empower you to cultivate? Dinner parties? Time with your children? A moment of reprieve from the cacophony of devices we all know all too well? If any of your stuff helps you connect with loved ones—or yourself—perhaps it deserves to stick around.

BRING ON THE PURGE

For everything else? That's where the purge comes in. Getting rid of stuff, or "purging," as it's more commonly known, isn't simply throwing things away, although it gets a bad rap as such. Purging is about agency. It's about deciding for yourself what is important to you and how your surroundings reflect your values. (Remember what we said about bringing home stuff you're just going to throw away?) Purging takes many different forms, but there are essentially two main ways to go about it: an all-day sort-a-thon or a steady series of smaller actions. For some, it can be energizing to see a giant pile form on the living room floor; it makes you realize how much space you've been handing over to things, and how much better life would be if that pile simply vanished. Others find it better to tackle the job piece by piece on a daily or weekly basis, or else they find themselves overwhelmed. You don't want to give up before even getting started!

GET THROUGH IT

Whatever your purge style, remember that getting rid of stuff is a means to an end, not the end itself. Set up separate piles and bins for donation, recycling, trash, and items you want to keep. Make it fun by playing music and ordering takeout, or make it an ascetic experience by depriving yourself of all earthly joys until it's over and done. Regardless, remember to take Paula Mallis's words from chapter 1 to heart: "Every time you declutter, you're dumping the unconscious." Purging isn't about disposing, trashing, or deleting—it's about purpose, about unearthing the reasons we keep what we keep and getting clear of what's silently holding us back.

WORK TOGETHER

Admittedly, a clearing out consensus can be hard to reach. How do you get people on board? Ask if an item should go on display in a shadowbox; if it's really meaningful, you'll enjoy seeing it on your wall at all times. If someone balks at the idea, maybe it's not so sentimental after all. Or put things in a box and mark it with the date, then see if you even think about what's inside for three months. If you forget about it, purge it all; if you went back to it, find ways to better incorporate its contents into your home. Try a modified version for kids: Designer and influencer Caitlin Flemming has her husband take their children to the park, then hides excess or unloved toys. If after a few weeks the kids haven't asked about them, she knows she can let them go.

Minimalist Mission

Karla Gallardo is one half of Cuyana, a San Francisco–based women's apparel brand that helped spark the lean-closet revolution with its exquisite, time-honored basics. So it's no surprise that she's landed in our chapter on living with just the right amount of stuff. To craft an inspiring home that reflects this spirit, the businesswoman worked with Lauren Nelson of Lauren Nelson Design. "Lauren designs through the lens of how to make a space feel comfortable and inviting while still representing the person. We worked together to design the entire space from scratch, with most of the pieces made custom by local artisans. The space was built around a juxtaposition of marble, brass, and light oak for a bright and airy feeling," Gallardo says.

Gallardo and her husband bought the San Francisco home just after getting married. The three-bedroom space has an open floor plan, which Gallardo cites as one of the features she adores about it. "I love big, light-filled spaces. The home is perfect for gathering with friends and family," she says. "The design elements aren't too trendy; it embodies a timeless aesthetic to see us through year through year. It marries clean Scandinavian inspiration with a modern feel."

When asked about her decorating approach, Gallardo says, "My personal approach to interior design is the same philosophy that Cuyana was founded on: surrounding myself with fewer but better things that have meaning." To add some balance to her busy work and family life, she makes sure everything has a distinct place. "I need a home that is designed to work with my busy schedule so that I never have to second-guess anything," she explains. "I depend on functional details and a curated aesthetic."

Gallardo says that the soul of the home may be the kitchen, but she really loves the whole space for entertaining. "Our entire home is designed for hosting, which is why there is a lot of table space everywhere." The light and airy dining room is grounded by a matte-black accent—an Innermost Circus pendant. A royal-blue credenza custom designed by Lauren Nelson Designs steals the show in the dining room, while one of Gallardo's favorite pieces hangs above it. "It's the first piece my husband and I invested in after we got married," she says. "It's artwork that we fell in love with during a trip to Australia at Aquabumps—a photography studio that celebrates early-morning beach life. Its calming light-blue and turquoise tones became the centerpiece around which we built the rest of the main space."

"I love to gather around the island in the kitchen over a bottle of wine with dear friends," Gallardo says, and we can easily see why. With stand-out pieces like bar stools from the Danish Design Store and hanging beads from Hudson Grace, the kitchen is pretty breathtaking, and makes for a perfectly minimalist hub for a modern family.

*So calming and serene—
the use of blue tones in this
home really sets a scene.*

PREVIOUS SPREAD / WIDE OPEN SPACES

Custom-designed by Lauren Nelson, a perfect pair of pale-blue couches creates a serene relaxation center in Gallardo's open floor plan. Two matching marble-and-wood coffee tables (also from Nelson) anchor the space, staggered to create visual interest, while a striking black-and-white photograph injects a little drama into the peaceful sanctuary.

OPPOSITE / MINIMALIST CUISINE

A subdued palette of whites and grays make for a dreamy retreat of a kitchen.

ABOVE, LEFT / THE HEART OF THE HOME

Gallardo's kitchen is a vision in blue, and one of her favorite spaces in the home. Pops of the home's trademark deep turquoise tie it to the adjacent dining and living areas.

ABOVE, RIGHT / FINISHING TOUCHES

"Warm, minimalist, functional"—that's how Gallardo describes her home. The towering candlesticks add a welcome touch of glam, while a ceramic vase of botanicals softens up all the Scandinavian-influenced clean angles and hard-lined surfaces.

PREVIOUS SPREAD / MUTED CONTRAST
The black-and-white theme of the entryway plays out in this tabletop vignette with dark speckled and striped vases over a slab of black-and-white marble. Even the florals match! In the living space the tried-and-true palette gets a sophisticated twist with the oak-and-black color combo.

ABOVE, LEFT / EVERYTHING IN ITS PLACE
To add some balance to her busy work and family life, Gallardo makes sure everything has a distinct place. A tidy and bright collection of board books and toys makes a cheerful nook for her son.

ABOVE, RIGHT / BABY'S FIRST HERMES
The nursery highlights include an Oeuf dresser (used as a changing table) and a crib—with an Hermès

throw tossed over it, no less. A muted, soothing palette is pepped up by a festive garland.

OPPOSITE / CRAFTING AN OASIS
A cozy-looking bedroom if we ever did see one! A pair of black-and-brass sconces angle in over a bed dressed in blush and shades of gray, while a classic George Nelson lamp rules over the scene.

We love a home that is so perfectly attuned to who its owners are as a family.

Two Takes on Letting It Go

ADVICE FROM WIEBKE LIU, BLISSHAUS

A former VP of marketing who founded sustainable-kitchen empire Blisshaus, Wiebke Liu has harnessed her analytical skills to develop smarter, more sustainable ways of living for her clients. To say that she's an organizational expert is an understatement: She approaches crowded pantries with the efficiency of an engineer and the artistry of an architect. Her solutions are foundational—not merely cosmetic—and her swelling client list reflects that.

QUESTION POSSESSIONS

Liu starts with the pantry—"pretty pantries with a purpose," she calls them, and goes from there. She asks clients to determine which category each items belong to: beauty, utility, or memory. "My nemesis is Tupperware," says Liu with a laugh. She starts by looking at the established workflow of the space and then goes micro, trying to solve for different pain points along the way. She believes more is more, with some projects using up to 100 different labeled and sized jars for organizing everything from lentils to flour. "The kitchen is the training wheels for what you do in the rest of your home."

PURGE WITH A PURPOSE

Liu's team sorts drawers and cabinets by color and material, then she encourages clients to "shop" their own spaces for the things worth keeping. "Most utensil drawers are a shitshow," says Liu. "You need to streamline the process of cooking while minimizing clutter—but it's not all or nothing." In other words, you *can* have stuff out on the counter, but "Don't let it take up physical space when it has an emotional footprint," Liu warns. "And recognize that you'll grow out of loving some things."

MAKE IT A FAMILY AFFAIR

Liu preaches mindfulness and ease of use, not minimalism. This includes simple things like moving dishes to a lower drawer so that kids can reach them without breaking anything, or storing plates closer to a dishwasher. Identify the tasks each person does most often in that space, then maximize for efficiency. "It's not about whittling down the way a photo stylist does," she counsels. "You really have to think about functionality."

ADVICE FROM CAITLIN FLEMMING, BLOGGER & DESIGNER

Growing up with an antiques dealer for a mother, Caitlin Flemming's M.O. as both a parent and an interior designer was to not baby-proof her house, instead keeping her stylish abode decidedly adult friendly. "I'm not going to change the way I live for my kids," says the San Francisco–based influencer and designer whose lifestyle blog, Sacramento Street, offers a wealth of inspiration spanning fashion, design, parenting, and more. It's a bold philosophy that few would dare attempt, but Flemming makes it work through a mixture of proactive choices and sheer willpower.

QUESTION POSSESSIONS

Flemming's mother instilled in her a reverence for quality over quantity. Knowing where to spend and where to save has been one of the designer's most important life lessons; for instance, she saved for years for her first major purchase, a Turkish rug she still cherishes to this day. Flemming honed her chic minimalist style during the years she spent creating a gracious space in a studio apartment. The challenge she faced was needing to be incredibly selective when considering buying any piece of furniture, art, or almost anything for the home. To avoid feeling overwhelmed by stuff, she tried to get rid of one piece for every one purchased.

PURGE WITH A PURPOSE

The mother of two has baskets for toys (a growing collection, as any parent knows), and twice a year the entire family does a purge, getting rid of anything and everything that doesn't pass muster. ("I thought about doing a no-shopping pledge, but couldn't commit," Flemming confesses.)

MAKE IT A FAMILY AFFAIR

Flemming says it is important to have systems in place that make it easy to instill and act on a set of values for the whole family. Remember those toy baskets? Toys have to go in them each evening. And mom has to stay in line as well. "I take fifteen or twenty minutes at the end of every day to make sure the house is clean and ready for the next day. I don't want to set a precedent that messy is the norm," she explains. Setting that example is important for Flemming's children to see. "Having a place for everything is so important, but such a struggle," she says with a laugh.

Gilty Pleasure

Jeet Sohal's Hancock Park family home is a throwback to Hollywood's Golden Era—but don't let that fool you into thinking it's just for show. Sohal is the founder of the fine jewelry line Bare Collection and mother to three boys, and her home reflects a gorgeous maximalism, as well as a studied approach to design for function as well as form.

Located on a picturesque street in a family friendly neighborhood, this "forever home" presented a unique set of challenges that Sohal took head on, designing the space herself, with a little guidance from her mother. "I've got a good sense of how I want things to look—a good base of design knowledge from years of obsession with architecture and industrial and furniture design—and an amazing mom who has a great eye and always asks the right questions that take me to the next level."

Sohal approached the project with patience and a more-is-more attitude, harnessing her design obsessions to create a space that is dazzling in its approachability. For example, the Dieter Rams-designed 606 Universal Shelving System in the library was one of the first things Sohal ever saved on Pinterest, years before it became her first major purchase here.

"I love to live in a space and determine what my needs are before I begin. Once I've determined the function, it's easy for me to come up with an efficient and beautiful flow and populate the space with objects that support that flow," she says. "Unfortunately, figuring out my needs takes time! That means that a space is effectively empty until it's not."

The end result (though the space is still evolving) is a stately, layered residence that respects the home's storied history (John Barrymore was a previous owner) while meeting the family of five's very contemporary needs. Luckily, achieving that didn't require extensive renovations. "After taking care of the basics, we added east-facing French doors in the family room to let in some morning light, and reconfigured the boys' bedroom and bathroom to better accommodate the three of them," says Sohal. "We also repurposed some of the laundry spaces in the house. When we moved in, there were two huge laundry rooms and six built-in ironing boards! We took one of the laundry rooms and converted it to a home office for myself with the help of designer and general contractor Tracy McCormick."

It's a skillful balance that Sohal has become accustomed to striking with aplomb, combining the intimacy of her jewelry design work with the passion and drive to decorate her own home. When asked about how she bridges her work and interior-design sensibilities, she says: "Fine jewelry is purchased to mark a moment: an achievement, a life milestone, an emotional development, a transition, etc. It's a forever purchase. I have the same approach to every object in our house: research, evaluation, and acquisition. Ninety-nine percent of what I buy will be in my life for its useful life, sometimes even longer, so I give myself time to make sure it's something I'm in love with. But I still have impulse purchases, after all—we can all believe in love at first sight!"

Art can make or break the room. The pieces in Jeet's stately home feel personal and inject a playful tone.

PREVIOUS SPREAD / WORTH THE WAIT

A painting by Danvy Pham rests on the mantel in the stunning living room, while a Vladimir Kagan floating sofa is set across from two vintage Arredamenti Corallo chairs and a Silas Seandel table. Pham's piece is one of Sohal's favorites. "I've been obsessed with it since I was in my 20s, but Danvy Pham—the artist and my dear friend—refused to sell," Sohal tells us. "Thankfully, 15 years later, reason finally prevailed and we got to be one of her first clients."

OPPOSITE / STAYING TRUE TO THE ORIGINAL

A peek at the formal dining room and its detailed wood paneling shows the home's truly breathtaking craftsmanship. Luckily, Sohal didn't have to do a ton of renovations, as the home was already nicely restored. "The previous owner did most of the difficult restoration work on the wood paneling and leaded glass windows," she shares.

ABOVE, LEFT / TASTEFUL TEATIME

At Sohal's, it's always a stylish mix. Dainty porcelain tea cups feel at home among crystals and vividly patterned floor pillows.

ABOVE, RIGHT / DECADENT DRESSING

Next to the master bedroom, the dramatic (and roomy) dressing room is quite a stunner, painted in mint green and appointed with shaggy fur throws.

ABOVE / MAKING PLAYTIME STYLISH

The landing leading into the playroom sports a photo of Sohal's youngest son, taken for a class project. A vivid California Blue by Benjamin Moore bedecks the playroom walls, while a tent and Waldorf-style play kitchen provide endless entertainment.

OPPOSITE PAGE, TOP / ALL TOGETHER NOW

Sohal and her three sons hanging out in the backyard, which features a full kitchen and a stunning pool. The home's outdoor space is packed with potential for entertaining.

OPPOSITE PAGE, BOTTOM / THRIFT ENVY

A midcentury headboard (a Craigslist score) pairs nicely with the blue wall. Of the home's striking colors, Sohal says, "I needed a bold palette to keep the space cohesive."

This home exudes elegance and maximalism while still feeling family friendly.

OPPOSITE / SHELFIE GOALS

"The shelving system is Vitsœ, designed by Dieter Rams," Sohal says. "I screengrabbed it on a now-defunct blog focused on home libraries and shelving systems. Years later, I was introduced to the West Coast director of Vitsœ, Rob Fissmer, at dinner and geeked out. . . . When we moved, it was my first major home purchase!"

ABOVE LEFT / OUT OF THIS WORLD

The boys' room is painted in Gentleman's Gray by Benjamin Moore and features a handsome bunk bed. Star Wars–themed wall art ups the playfulness factor.

ABOVE RIGHT / A ROYAL LOUNGE

Next to the kitchen space, the purple-themed family room—outfitted with a Roche Bobois Mah Jong sofa in Missoni fabric—is where Sohal finds her family hanging out the most. "The space is bright, and I'm always doing food prep or cooking," nearby, she notes, "and the kids are always playing or reading there."

STAGGER HEIGHTS When staging a #aesthetic shelf situation, place your goods with an eye for variety. Lay books down as well as standing them on end, and use them as platforms for pretty objects. Fill in space with taller items for a more robust panorama, and let a plant trail between shelves.

THE ART OF THE SHELFIE

"Shelfie" joined the popular vernacular when the onslaught of cute shelf vignettes on social media became too engaging to ignore. We all know and love a neatly arranged, thoughtfully color-coordinated, and prettily posed Insta-moment—and the shelfie is all of those things, plus a great way to display all that stuff we've been working through in this chapter. If you're looking to get that double tap, the shelfie is your golden ticket.

PICK A PRETTY READING LIST Metallic type, perfectly worn classics, uncut pages—don't feel guilty about having books meant solely for display. It helps to keep other items in the same colorway, like this limited-palette combo. As for the debate over turning in the spines for an even more neutral palette, you do you.

INCORPORATE IMAGES

Photos and other art are the ideal backbone for a prime shelfie. Framed or unframed, they provide a backdrop for the different objects and collectibles you want to keep on display. It's also easy to switch them up and out, moving in new pieces with fresh colors, textures, and graphic elements.

INTERJECT LIFE—AND LIGHT

Whether trailing vines, perfectly pruned leafage, or adorable baby succulents, greenery breathes literal life into an unassuming tableau. Similarly, candles are a great way to sneak in a few more elements: consider brass, glass, or ceramic jars (with or without cute labels); candles in surprising shapes; and, of course, fun candlesticks and candelabras.

AT HOME WITH PLANTS *Ian Drummond & Kara O'Reilly* B|O

the LONNY *home* B|O

HEAP ON THE CURIOS

Shelves aren't just for books, people. They're also the perfect home for a budding collection, or objects with a quiet theme. A lot of people think that these extras need to make sense or speak to a personal passion, but sometimes form really does trump function! Likewise, a vase or bowl can make a statement all on its own—it's not nonsensical simply because it's empty. Just put it out and see how it feels.

POLAROID

NAKED CAKES • *Lyndel Miller* B|O

Easeful Elegance

Elettra Wiedemann and her husband, actor Caleb Lane, recently welcomed a daughter to their home in Brooklyn's historic Fort Greene neighborhood. The cookbook author and former model has turned the classic brownstone into a cozy family home that spans multiple floors, a collected space fueled by a love of traditional furnishings and punctuated by the odd heirloom.

"I am actually terrible at decorating and very impatient," she shares. "For the first year that I lived here, this place looked like an empty loft. I hardly had any furniture. Then, slowly, I inherited family heirlooms and found decorative pillows we loved, and it started coming together." The thing is, there's real merit to this slow-and-steady approach: Rather than frantically filling the void of a new home with the latest trend pieces, Wiedemann lived with her space for a while, letting magical, just-right, and one-of-a-kind decor pieces fill it up in due time. In this way, minimalism can be a kind of gateway—less of a staunch aesthetic, and more of a means to a peaceful and curated end.

The pared-down-yet-pretty result also manages to support the family's daily priorities. "Our only rule is that nothing be precious—we want things to feel easy," she continues. "If something gets stained, throw it in the wash; if the dogs run around and track mud into the house, it's not a big deal. I don't want to have stuff that feels like I have to hover over it to protect it." For Wiedemann, that means a lot of slipcovers and, oddly enough, a lot of white paint. (Easy indeed, but not exactly forgiving.)

Wiedemann has lived in the home for three years, but owned it for six. Before moving in and making it her own, she spent nine months renovating the property, which was originally built in 1890. "There are so many original details in the house that I fell in love with, like the moldings, old gas lamp fixtures, and old fireplaces. The second I walked into the house, despite it being kind of a wreck, I fell completely in love." To Wiedemann's knowledge, only two other families had lived in the home before it came into her possession, and the time warp was real. "The entire house had

to be renovated, especially the things behind walls like electricity and plumbing," she says. "The infrastructure of the house was a major focus of the work; the top floor was gutted and given a completely new layout. Otherwise, the layout of the house is as it was and maybe always has been."

She describes the home as "minimalist, cozy, and comfortable." Its traditional uprightness and crisp airiness—warmed up by antiques, simple yet voluminous greenery, and a few looser, more organic choices—

We love this home because it preserves history and charm, and it feels minimal yet warm.

help make the home a haven for others, too. "I like to entertain, so having a space that feels comfortable and welcoming to guests is important to me." Some of the most eye-catching items are antiques not from family, but from the house itself. The stained-glass piece that rests on the dining room mantel was recovered from the basement, and the carved Victorian armchairs in the sitting room had been left behind, too. "I don't really follow trends," says Wiedemann. "I just like to have things in my house hold a memory or tell a story."

PREVIOUS SPREAD / SIMPLE & SERENE

There's no denying the house's stunning historical accents, so when decorating Wiedemann used a light hand. A wooden ladder—a family heirloom—rests against a wall in the dining room, lending a rustic touch to an otherwise stately space.

OPPOSITE / UPDATING KEEPSAKES

The sofas in the living room (like many items throughout the home) are inherited pieces. Understated white slipcovers bring them into the modern era, assisted by the strong lines of the square coffee table and sophisticated pale-turquoise palette.

ABOVE / AN IDYLLIC PERCH

The brownstone's small porch leads from the kitchen to a sizable backyard, where Wiedemann's dogs get some exercise and the family unwinds en plein air. "I love the patio and garden, especially sitting outside, reading, or laying in the hammock in the summertime," she says.

We love the juxtaposition of styles seen throughout the home. These traditional, stately chairs coupled with a bright rug and earthy side table really stand out.

OPPOSITE / TWO'S COMPANY
A pair of chairs that came with the home sit against the wall, anchored by a One Kings Lane rug. This room's bright but limited palette—consisting of electric oranges and pinks, offset by neutral cream—makes the antique furniture feel fresh.

ABOVE / A FOODIE'S RETREAT
Naturally, the kitchen is the place where Wiedemann spends most of her time—whether that's cooking or writing for her site, *Impatient Foodie*

When asked if her profession informs her decorating choices, Wiedemann explains, "I think food is a fun but also a messy profession, so it probably informs my choice to have everything in the house be low maintenance and not precious."

FOLLOWING SPREAD / RICH VIGNETTES
A stained-glass window rescued from the basement acts as art, leaning above an ornate stone fireplace, while decorative pillows and a Fender guitar make for a lovely rock-and-roll moment.

Four Ways to Create Functional Storage

1 GO WITH OPEN SHELVING

Open shelving is not for the faint of heart. It takes time and careful consideration, not to mention planning. Start by figuring out what pieces you really need, which things look good together, and how best to group them. When arranging, keep purely decorative or rarely used objects on higher shelves so everyday items stay in reach. A color-harmonized collection of containers and vessels allows you to incorporate different textures and shapes for a dynamic display.

2 CONCEAL AND CORRAL

In the kitchen, there are a multitude of chic options for hiding away all your less-than-chic necessities. Take a page out of Wiebke Liu's book (see page 86) and decant your pantry staples into lidded jars and containers for easy access—and to avoid a hot mess of labels. Or lean into the label look, displaying pantry goods with the prettiest of packaging. Likewise, you can make a display of handsome kitchen tools with a caddy (and never get them stuck in a drawer again).

Storage is a pain point for pretty much everybody. If you have it, it can be hard to figure out how to use it well, and if you live in cramped quarters, it can mean ugly solutions that feel slapdash. We want to help you create easy-to-use storage solutions that scale—functional ideas that can be applied to your starter apartment or your first family home and then grow with you.

3 DISPLAY IT AS ART

Another option, especially if you have sentimental pieces, is to make artful displays. Try a shadowbox for porcelain or glassware, with room for a few framed illustrations or little paintings. Baskets can be art as well as storage, and the right hook—say, one made of gorgeous brass—can turn a hanging linen dish towel into a work of art. Antique silverware, hand-carved wooden spoons, and other unique utensils can all be elevated with an eye for the most pleasing arrangements.

4 PUT UP AN ORG SYSTEM

A wall-mounted organization system keeps your most-used tools within reach. Function, not form, is your real concern here; try storing pieces vertically on a customizable pegboard display, or install overhead racks for pots and pans. There are molded plastic options as well that can create a different vibe, while wall-mounted office caddies work wonders in places outside the home office. There are many price-point options for this kind of storage—plus, it's easy to DIY.

No-Fuss Chic

Si Mazouz has lived in a fairy-tale-like string of locales: Morocco, provincial France, and stateside in historic North Carolina and bustling San Francisco. Outfitted with treasures from each spot, her San Francisco home is every bit as dreamy as you'd expect, but it also displays a casual restraint—an uncomplicated minimalism that helps each curio and collectible stand out. It's also filled with one-of-a-kind pieces Mazouz built or modified herself. "My decorating philosophy is rather simple: Follow no preset rule and, above all, follow your intuition," says Mazouz.

A childhood spent in Rabat, Morocco, informs the author and design blogger's carefully curated aesthetic and cross-cultural inclinations. "I quit my job in marketing in France when we moved to the United States," Mazouz remembers. "Since my girls did not speak one word of English and my husband was traveling extensively, I decided to take a break from work to be more available to my kids while we were settling in North Carolina." Her blog, *French By Design,* was born of her Etsy shop, where she curated and sold vintage decor and furniture. Social media is where Mazouz shares snippets of her space, much to

the delight of her forty-thousand-plus followers. "The living room's built-in bookcase gets a lot of attention and questions," she says.

The living room holds some of Mazouz's most prized possessions, among them her Gervasoni white linen sofa ("It's so comfortable and easy to clean") and a vintage Beni Ourain rug she purchased in the souks of Marrakesh. A flair for DIY is also on view: Mazouz built her coffee table using scaffolding planks left in her back yard in Provence. "I made some raised gardening beds for my girls to teach them about growing vegetables, and made this low table on casters as a temporary coffee table for our living room. Now, I'm emotionally attached to it. Although it's all dangling and the surface is not straight, I wouldn't trade it for a designer piece!" She used the leftover wood to build a large statement mirror, which now leans against a wall in the master bedroom. "It has moved with us three times, and movers hate me for it because the structure is not sturdy like manufactured ones, but it's still here with us! I love its imperfections and the 'raw' look and texture of it," she says.

Many of the furnishings in the home, like the wood dining table, have traveled with Si from city to city and country to country. Throughout, a theme emerges. Each room is pulled together, but nothing is over-styled. "I don't like symmetry in interior design, and I don't like 'sets,'" Si says. "I am also a vintage chair addict, so mixing and matching my dining chairs made total sense around our dining table."

All in all, Si's light-drenched, whitewashed home feels spare yet inviting, pared back but not bereft. Enlivened with designer pieces and international scores, it's both homey and curated, equally elegant and chill.

There is something just so approachable and inviting about this Scandi-inspired abode.

PREVIOUS SPREAD /
FADE TO (NEAR) BLACK

The star of the bedroom is the wall color—
Alpine Trail by Behr Marquee—a hue so
dark green it's almost black, and a real
departure from the rest of the home's stark
white. And there are many other gems in this
space. The boutis-style French quilt adorning
the bed is a farmers' market find from
Provence, and an Eames low table adds
designer style.

OPPOSITE / BOOKCASE BEAUTY

Minimalism doesn't mean ridding your
home of collections—it just requires finding
clever ways of holding them at bay. Here,
a boatload of brightly colored books
gets contained and subdued by a built-in
bookcase. The leather pouf is from Morocco.

ABOVE LEFT / TO DYE FOR

Among Mazouz's custom projects is her
hand-dyed hallway runner. "It was an old
runner rug we had bought in Morocco," she
tells us. "I found a website with a step-by-step
tutorial on overdyeing wool rugs. I tried it in
my backyard, and voilà!"Mazouz's golden
retriever, Daisy, makes frequent appearances
on the French By Design Instagram
account and even has her own hashtag,
#lifewithmissdaisy.

ABOVE RIGHT / MAXIMUM ORDER

As in the rest of the home, the covetable
furnishings in the office are a mix of high
and low. The desk is IKEA, the Boucherouite
rug is from Secret Berbère, the wall
organizer is the Vitra Uten.Silo, and the
industrial chair, wall lamp (a Kaiser-idell from
Fritz Hansen), and tulip chair are all thrifted.
With everything in its place, it provides a
perfect blank slate for creative work.

ABOVE / SUN-DRENCHED MINIMALISM
Sunlight floods the living room—it's one of Mazouz's favorite features of the home. There's simple style everywhere, with a casually thrown sheepskin warming up a vintage rattan chair and scaled-back accessories on the coffee table. The fireplace setup is stunning—candles upon candles—with a cheeky disco ball on the floor.

OPPOSITE / PLAYING FAVORITES
The living room is the site of some of Si's most treasured pieces—the Gervasoni sofa, the vintage Beni Ourain rug, and her DIY coffee table. Hanging to the left of the sofa is a floor lamp by Flos.

FOLLOWING SPREAD / TONE ON TONE
The stark bathroom gets a sophisticated tone with tile in varying shades of gray, while the room's shelves are slightly less minimal than the rest of the abode. Back in the living room, the bookshelf is packed with personality—how sweet are the monkey and the Eames House Bird from Vitra?

We love how her personal items are styled in a way that feels useful but also beautiful and elevated.

TOM FORD

TRAVAIL DU BOIS

MAROC

TANGER

Four Ways to Update Boring Furniture

1 ADD EMBELLISHMENTS

Sometimes a chair is just a chair until you add a little something extra. Appliqués and trimmings in wood or vinyl can really enliven a mundane seating situation, or you can draw inspiration from more classical techniques—trimmings along the seat, or piping around a back cushion—and let your imagination run wild from there. Unexpected treatments, like wrapping legs and seat backs in multicolored yarn, can be a fun way to personalize a piece.

2 MAKE A SWAP

Switching out the legs of a chair or sofa is an easy undertaking that doesn't require extensive skill—or budget—and it can pack a visual punch. Choose from traditional wood styles, or try more contemporary powder-coated steel legs. If your piece came with accents like tufting or nailhead trim, mix it up with different finishes and contrasting colors—or remove them completely. Alternatively, you can embellish the piece with a design made of wood scraps and trimmings for a custom look.

Tired of a hard-working plain piece? Recently inherited a lovely hand-me-down in need of a real refresh? Whether you're overcome with a sudden urge to refurbish or you're known to trawl Craigslist for vintage or save gems from the street (we see you, budget-savvy city-dwellers) you'll want to check out these DIY tips for giving less-than-perfect pieces a little TLC.

3 TREAT THE SURFACE

You don't have to play it as it lays, at least not when it comes to your furniture. Treat an unimpressive surface with any of a variety of stains, paint, or cosmetic distressing techniques. You can also experiment with a stenciled pattern, or try a process like gilding, decoupage, or wax transfer to get a one-of-a-kind effect. It's also easy to paint or treat the frame of your favorite chair or sofa, and remember: You don't have to take on every step of this process yourself.

4 SOFTEN IT UP

Hard angles got you down? Take the piece to an upholsterer to have it redone using one of your favorite fabrics, or even a vintage rug. (Local design magazines can guide you, and a lot of DIYers-for-hire are on Instagram nowadays.) Or save time and budget with a store-bought slipcover. For a look that can change with the seasons, use a faux fur throw or animal hide to add cold-weather cushion and comfort, then swap for linens and lightweight knits during the warmer months.

Neon Dream

The first time Manish Arora set eyes on his future home in Paris's bohemian Canal Saint-Martin neighborhood, he knew he had to have it—and destroy it. "I thought: This is it," he says. "And my next thought was: I need to break as many walls as possible." This impulse to level the place—save for a load-bearing wall and the moldings and carved-marble fireplaces so typical of Parisian prewar apartments—wasn't the knee-jerk reaction of someone with an outsize creative complex, but simply a yearning to flood the space with natural light. "I cannot live in the dark," the New Delhi–born fashion designer says.

For those familiar with Arora's aesthetic, that will hardly come as a surprise. This is, after all, the man who took the fashion industry by storm in 2007 by becoming the first designer of Indian descent to present a collection—full of high-concept, rainbow-spectrum ready-to-wear showstoppers—at Paris Fashion Week. Using the intricate beading and handmade artisanal techniques from his native country with the immaculate tailoring and avant-garde silhouettes of his adopted France, Arora quickly won critical raves and high-profile fans including Kate Moss, Rihanna, and Katy Perry. Reviewers have used phrases such as "sugar rush" and "cuckoo for Cocoa Puffs" to describe his runway shows, which reference everything from art deco to K-pop to Burning Man, all seen through a Bollywood lens. So, clearly his home was never going to be minimal or moody. Instead, it's a shrine to the interplay of color, the transformative properties of light, and the juxtaposition of palatial fixtures with worldly tchotchkes. Or, to use Arora's own words, "I'm scared of too much white."

Much like Arora's fashion sensibility, the apartment overflows with theatrical touches. The bedroom evokes Sunset Boulevard, with an entire wall devoted to 1930s-style gold mosaic mirrors picked up at an antiques shop on Paris's Boulevard de Strasbourg. "I planned it in such a way that the sun hits the wall in the morning and flashes the whole room," the designer says, clearly delighted by his Midas-touch craftiness. "It's all gold light when I wake up."

Arora holds court in the lounge amid his ever-expanding array of Japanese and Russian figurines, his collection of kitschy plastic food scored at a market in Tokyo, and his prized artwork: a wondrous oversize sticker mosaic by Chinese artist Ye Hongxing. This space is a work in progress, steadily updated with souvenirs from Arora's travels and providing constant inspiration for a man who thrives on visual companionship: "I feel comfortable in the clutter. I feel strange and scared in an empty space."

Yet despite the neon tones and the whirlwind of international influences, Arora's home is surprisingly zen. To achieve its airy exuberance, he embraced linear forms, clean colorblocking, and immense amounts of light. "I try to avoid bulky furniture," he says. "Everything is see-through or lean and thin so that light is reflected in as many places as possible." The result? An over-the-top oasis for a color-happy provocateur.

Splashes of bold color and print beautifully rep this homeowner's vivid style.

PREVIOUS SPREAD /
A FLOATING DINNER PARTY

Arora's cheery dining area is brimming with focal points, including a decidedly groovy black-and-white runner and a trio of rimmed aluminum lamps. The 1960s Perspex-and-wood dining table appears to float in midair, surrounded by an eclectic assortment of seats that includes Paris flea market finds as well as design icons like an original rope-edged Eames and a Gaetano Pesce Spring Chair.

OPPOSITE / WELCOME WAGON

The sensory assault begins at the door, thanks to a freewheeling mural of fish-scale patterns, cartoon hearts, and a bubbly

typographic treatment by Parisian street artist Rude. "When I enter my house, I need to see a blast of color," Arora explains. "I need to say, O-KAY! I'm back." A robot dog and a neon-pink poodle sculpture set a whimsical tone, greeting everyone who enters.

ABOVE LEFT / LAYING IT ON THICK

It took six coats of paint to achieve this super-opaque effect—a bold contrast to the white herringbone parquet floors. The lineup of dolls from Arora's Russian and Japanese collections complements the pink backdrop—we love the wit of the matching radiator.

ABOVE RIGHT / THE MAN HIMSELF

Manish Arora stands in the doorway of his bedroom, modeling a vivid sweater from his Spring 2013 collection.

OPPOSITE / SEAT IN THE CLOUDS

Arora insists that only upbeat entertainment be screened on his home projector, which means that *Tom and Jerry* cartoons are shown in frequent rotation. A secondhand sofa upholstered in a Manish Arora textile inspired by the sky at Burning Man brings a psychedelic feeling to the lounge.

ABOVE / CUSTOM DELIGHTS

"The kitchen is the smallest part of my apartment, and there's a very good reason for that: I don't cook," says Arora. Still, the visual feast continues with made-to-measure cabinetry conceptualized by Arora's architect, Antoine Pradels, and a bespoke wall of prismatic glass panels handmade in India.

ABOVE LEFT / COTTON CANDY

Arora considers his sleeping quarters to be the calmest space in the house. A stag skull and antlers add a surprisingly rustic touch, and vibrant floral bedding from the designer's collection plays off a '30s-inspired gold mirror on the opposite wall.

ABOVE RIGHT / HOT-PINK STREAK

"Bourgeois decadence" was the order of the day in the bathroom, where a painted rose-pink claw-foot tub sits on concrete tiles from Petit Pan. The walls are painted yellow up to waist height, bordered by a contrasting pink trim. "It was difficult to explain to my architect that I wanted orange walls with pink on top; or green, blue, and yellow in one room," Arora says. "But this is how I live. It's an extension of my work."

OPPOSITE / ON THE MANTEL

Indian mythological and religious figures sit atop the carved-marble fireplace—one of the few original details Arora left intact after embarking on an extensive renovation to bring more light into the space.

This home has such an artful approach—and so much personality and vibrancy!

CHAPTER THREE

Seeking Your Inspiration

"Inspiration" has never been easier to find than it is today. With Pinterest boards and Instagram pages for every passion, you could spend all day, every day immersed in ideal homes, optimized outfits, and gorgeous vacation spots. But is this endless stream of images really helpful? Or is it simply overwhelming?

*I*n this chapter we'll show how to get outside of your favorite feeds and find new influences, which is the first step in developing a uniquely "you" approach to design. And then we'll turn those influences into reality. After all, seeking out inspiration is one thing, but pulling off that tricky alchemy that turns a cute idea into an even cuter reality, whether that's a TV corner or book nook, let alone—egads!—a floor-to-ceiling kitchen renovation, well that can be pretty intimidating.

The fact of the matter is that there's no right or wrong way to approach your space. Take, for instance, Michael Woodcock and artist Lara Apponyi, who combine forces in the studio Work + Sea as well as in the eclectic yet pulled-together space that they share. Or check out the inspiring example of Carly Nance, co-founder of The Citizenry, whose business background wasn't at odds with her creative drive—and, in fact, actually helped her find new ways to make something of her passion for travel.

The point is, a good idea can strike you at any given time, and come in just about any shape or and size. You might find renewed meaning in your dad's old bird-watching memorabilia, or take a cue from the set design of your latest Netflix binge-watch. It's important not to assume that certain sources have "higher" or "lower" cultural value; the best spaces are true to their owners' interests and usually mesh the old with the new, the uptown with the downtown, the whimsical with the practical.

In the words of Siosi Design's Audi Culver, "Keep it simple, keep lots of plants, and be open to change and evolution." Read on for more ways to find and follow your inspirations.

GET OUT OF YOUR HOME—AND YOUR HEAD

Inspiration can strike anywhere and be applied in so many different contexts. The question is, how do you learn to trust your own taste? It starts with experience, and so getting out into the world is crucial. It's the step that turns your "Paris Is Always a Good Idea" bumper sticker into a collection of antique linens, a found portrait from a flea market near the Seine, or a grouping of antique *moutarde* jars. Seek out objects, palettes, architectural details, and textures that speak to your sensibility. At the end of the day, experience is the difference between *thinking* Paris is always a good idea and knowing it. A caveat: We're not suggesting that international travel is the only way to develop a sense of style. Wherever you are in the world, it's about seeing what makes a place special. Every region, every town has its own design vernacular that can be learned—and unlearned if it's not your cup of tea. (Perhaps Vegas is an acquired taste.)

LOG ON (BUT WITH INTENTION)

How do you express your style at home? Start by using the tools that are immediately available to you. Really engaging with Pinterest, for example, can be a great first step towards an informed way of interacting with the world. Create a moodboard of things that interest you and then break it down: Focus on colors that speak to you, shapes and textures you love, and whether or not you're drawn to bold patterns. Find historical references that inform your contemporary crushes and use online research and recommendations to make informed decisions about where to go and what to do once you get there. Then disconnect and live in the moment—give yourself permission to create your own meanings and to have your own experiences of a place, even if you (and everyone else) found it on Instagram.

CANCEL YOUR CATALOGS

It's tempting to flip through the latest offerings from one big-box retailer or another and think, "I'll have what she's having." But the key to personal style is unlocking your own latent creative potential. This means unlearning the lessons of design groupthink and stretching yourself to find new outlets and resources. All those coffee table books you've been collecting are good for more than just sitting pretty; set aside time to read them and find unexpected lessons and inspirations. Make your way through that backlog of home-decor magazines and tear out some of your favorite rooms, new designers, and maybe a bit of design history while you're at it. And go window shopping! Hit up a boutique design shop, antiques dealer, or design showroom and browse different finishes, fabrics, and even lighting schemes and dream room arrangements. Ask for fabric swatches so you can color match at home, or just keep them on hand for future reference.

At the end of the day, this chapter is all about finding and manifesting what makes you unique. Honing your eye through a diverse array of experiences will help you develop and refine your understanding of what you like—and how you want to live.

Bold Restraint

"We have different creative backgrounds, influences, and points of reference. But, when we strongly articulate a vision, it instantly becomes synchronized," say designer Michael Woodcock and artist Lara Apponyi, who combine forces in the studio Work + Sea. Offering interior styling and custom wallpapers that have garnered the attention of fashion visionary Jason Wu (who enlisted the duo for fabric designs), they offer a refreshing approach to color and pattern.

And the same thing can be said for the way the good friends and roommates infuse their tastes into their Los Angeles home. The Silver Lake space is full of vintage furniture pieces, eclectic art, and loud patterns that somehow meld into a look that's both elevated and conceptual. Mingling traditional patterns from around the globe and midcentury-modern staples with more utilitarian, self-made custom items and, of course, the irreverent wallpaper designs for which they're known, the pair considers themselves to be both minimalists and maximalists.

"We love minimalism for its honest use of modern technology to create structure, but we fully appreciate maximalism because we believe in celebrating unexpected connections, colors, and forms," the pair have explained. "Maximalism allows us to continually

explore and experiment, while also finding moments of humor."

The space's living room was one of the major selling points for them. "The views from the living room, the garden, the concrete fireplace, and the light originally attracted us to the home," they say. And they've made it into a real mixing pot of seemingly disparate patterns—for example, vintage Missoni, Nigerian batik, and Turkish kilim, all in one room!—resulting in a playground of unfussy, unexpected, and insanely imaginative decor. "Our home was once described as 'an eclectic mix that feels at once haphazard and by design, weird but also elegant. It all just makes sense together.' We like that."

At the heart of the home is the idea of inspiration, which is very much fueled by how the two work together. "We make products, design interiors, and create art. These processes inform and infuse with everything we make or purchase for our space," the two recount. "As with all of our wallpapers, we dream up the idea then gather inspiration imagery." In their work, the pattern-obsessed pair reference a wide array of influences, ranging from 19th-century French painter Henri Rousseau to contemporary filmmaker Wes Anderson. Several textiles from their travels—including a hypertactile burgundy wall hanging in the living room and a silk Egyptian rug on a wall in Woodcock's bedroom—are near and dear statement pieces that act as cornerstones for color and print motifs around the home. Of his rug, Woodcock says, "I plan to keep it forever and possibly hand it down to my kids."

But where does inspiration begin? "Pick the right location in a climate that suits you," the pair advises. Surround yourself by objects, colors, furniture, fabrics, books, items that you love, that conjure positive memories, or that inspire you." We couldn't have said it better.

This home is so artful and specific—every nook feels like a burst of personality.

PREVIOUS SPREAD / STATELY YET WILD

A custom bookshelf with artwork by Apponyi provides a dynamic backdrop for a Batik snake pillow, a vintage Turkish rug, and a midcentury-modern coffee table. The concrete fireplace—bedecked with contemporary takes on Russian nesting dolls and other curios—makes a quiet focal point in the room's riot of color and pattern, while the shelves provide welcome symmetry.

OPPOSITE / SITTING PRETTY

Woodcock and Apponyi lounge in their living room. A midcentury daybed and bolster pillows reupholstered in Missoni fabric really steal the show, and a Serge Mouille floor lamp adds a sleek, industrial touch. Apponyi cites the tulu rug that hangs above the daybed as one of her favorite items in the home. "It was my first personal interior-design investment," she shares. "It holds a lot of significance for me." A chintzy gold Elvis necklace catches the light in one corner of the tapestry.

ABOVE LEFT / BY A THREAD

In a corner of the living room, a rope art piece by Opinion Ciatti hangs between a monochromatic purple painting and an Artemide Dioscuri floor globe.

ABOVE RIGHT / RAISING THE BAR

A vintage bar cart does double duty, keeping booze and glassware handy, while allowing cool labels and funky colors to become a part of the decor.

ABOVE / PUT AN EGG ON IT

A custom wallpaper design by Work + Sea welcomes guests upon entering the eclectic yet inviting dining room. "The dining-room wallpaper is called 'Breakfast in Bed.' It's a repeat made up of fried eggs and boobs, set against a simple stripe," they share. "We wanted to incorporate an egg into a wallpaper design, then the boobs got involved over breakfast one morning. The circular shapes and subject matter seemed to fit really well together." A pair of Danish midcentury walnut chairs and two Saarinen Tulip chairs surround a custom table; a George Nelson pendant hangs above.

OPPOSITE / SUPERSATURATED

In the kitchen, high-gloss IKEA cabinets boast a deep red hue, picked up from the vibrant color of the vintage tulu rug in the living room. This striking choice is complemented by a backsplash in dark green tile. When it comes to adding color to your space, Woodcock and Apponyi suggest "going with your first instinctual choice. Don't worry about going off it—pick the color you love today." Here, silver legs and fixtures amplify the futuristic effect, while another vintage rug lends a surprisingly traditional and warm touch.

OPPOSITE / IT'S ALL IN THE MIX
An incredible little nook includes Work + Sea wallpaper, a vintage vanity, a rug from Double Knot, and a Louis-style ghost chair. "This print is inspired by the work of Henri Rousseau and the atmosphere evoked by large-scale nature murals," Apponyi explains. The butt sculptures—part of a work called *Fair Trade*—above the mirror are also among Apponyi's favorites. "The artist encourages the collector to exchange your acquired butt for another art object, and so emphasizing the lack of importance in material goods. However my butts were given to me by the artist, Marie Vic, who is a very close friend, so I won't be exchanging them for anything!"

ABOVE / CURTAIN CALL
Apponyi's room is an artistic paradise. A BFGF Shop throw covers her bed, while Gravel & Gold boob pillows and two Noguchi lamps anchor it. A variegated *monstrera friedrichsthalii* hangs in one corner—because every bedroom needs a touch of greenery—and the bedside wall features a Conrad Frankel painting and a framed napkin from the Parker Palm Springs hotel.

Bold prints and colors combine in a visual medley of the pair's artistic interests and experiences.

Two Takes on Seeking Your Inspiration

ADVICE FROM TZE CHUN, UPRISE ART

Tze Chun is an artist, a curator, and the founder of Uprise Art, an online gallery that highlights original work from emerging and established artists. Chun's personal style is as artful as one would expect, influenced by her grandparents' homes in Singapore and Hong Kong. Her approach to decor feels like a conversation about artistry; Chun's own practice was based in dance, and her design sense provides a fluidity that enthralls.

INVEST WISELY

"What's most meaningful is the story behind a piece," Chun says. Asking about the maker as well as the work helps you discern what kind of emotional value it can bring into your home; find out how old the artist is, how long they've been practicing, and if they're self-taught. "You can't feel comfortable with a stranger in your house," says Chun. Pick only the pieces that have resounding stories as well as satisfying forms.

PLAN AHEAD

Unless you're purchasing a piece of art at a high price point, you should plan to acquire artworks based on your personal tastes. "Life is too short, and you only have so many walls," says Chun. "The art I buy evokes the experiences I have while traveling." Then, once you've purchased the work, don't be overly concerned with maintaining it, but do take steps to protect it as you can—frame it, if need be, and keep most pieces, regardless of medium, out of direct sunlight.

EMBRACE CHANGE & CHANCE

Chun uses art to tell different stories in different rooms. "Nothing is forever," she says. "People get nervous about placement, but moving things around is good." Moving your *self* around is also key! Travel informs your cultural palette, and new experiences can help you identify what excites you and sparks your imagination. And speaking of sparks, it's important to have that impulsive, emotional reaction to the works that come home with you—but also to sleep on it. "If you can't look at it for a full five minutes, imagine five years," says Chun.

ADVICE FROM CARLY NANCE, THE CITIZENRY

With a background in brand strategy and a passion for travel, The Citizenry founder Carly Nance created a hub for all her inspirations in one e-commerce platform, with a simple goal: to help consumers bring that well-traveled look home, without needing to go into major debt over airfare. Her first-ever travel purchase was a kantha quilt that she brought back from India; stowed away in its folds was the idea for The Citizenry.

INVEST WISELY

Nance says that one of the biggest mistakes travelers make is amassing too many knickknacks rather than saving for one big purchase. "Do your research ahead of time so you know what a place is known for," suggests Nance. This will also help you shop more authentically, making informed purchasing decisions rather than impulse buys. Tours and cultural experiences with craft as a focus are another great way to learn about a new culture and partake of it in a way that provides perspective.

PLAN AHEAD

As wonderful as it would be to have great experiences fall in your lap, Nance admits she leans heavily on social media during the planning phases of her trips. She uses Instagram not only as visual inspiration but also as a way to reach out to influencers in the areas she'll be visiting, getting their shopping recommendations. She also checks out "bucket list" articles that help her curate the most meaningful experiences.

EMBRACE CHANGE & CHANCE

Nance suggests controlling your expectations while traveling, focusing on what your one big purchase is going to be and why. "A home has to have quiet moments as well as loud pieces," she says. "Otherwise you'll end up with a 'theme y' space." Always ask what a product is made from, seeking the best materials, like alpaca throws, heavyweight linens, and thick leathers. Editing down and doing your research will also save time—a crucial resource when on the road. "Don't overthink it and don't overdo it," says Nance. "Anything you pick up can be art!"

Form Marries Function

Want to know the coolest couple in the Midwest? Meet Ivy Siosi and Audi Culver, the furniture designers and makers behind the brand Siosi Design. The pair live together in Bloomington, Indiana, where they share a massive studio and a tiny home, both filled with their inventive creations. While many makers gravitate to the coasts, Siosi shares, "Our community in Bloomington, with its charming big-little city vibes, appreciates our work and offers enough upward mobility for our business to grow." Another great reason to stay in Indiana? "Plentiful, sustainable hardwoods surround us."

For this couple, beauty in utility is a resounding theme, and their serious woodworking chops allow them to custom-make whatever they need, in whatever style they want. One look at the pair's creations and you'll swoon over their practical pieces with classic yet innovative shapes. Culver says, "We combine lifestyle with work, think about form and function, design based on everyday inspiration, and combine pragmatism with creativity." Siosi also names travel as one of her biggest sources of creative input: "Seeing the innovation that comes from different materials and means, artistic expression, and needs being met has always led to . . . great design ideas."

While it's empowering to have your main source of inspiration be what you can envision with your own eyes and make with your own hands, the home of Siosi and Culver—like any home—reflects a journey. "When I moved into this space, I had very little furniture—a few antiques from my grandma, a couple of odds and ends from my

sister, and that was about it," Culver shares. "When Ivy moved in, this apartment started to feel like home. She added her personality and finesse, and our aesthetics worked well together and have evolved over time."

Their DIY spirit doesn't stop at furniture. "We have done everything ourselves (other than major plumbing and electrical)," says Culver. "Ivy is the handiest person I know, truly a Jill-of-all-trades—she can fix your vehicle and then draw a schematic of what she just fixed so you can better understand the process." She adds, "I'm incredibly lucky that the love of my life is also a brilliant designer and handy lady." They're the landlords for their 1920s-era four-unit building, which allows them to make it the best it can be.

When it comes to the home's decor itself, Siosi says, "It's incredible how fast stuff accumulates. Our choices are just an attempt at clearing out, donating, and simplifying some of that 'stuff.' What's left is sentimental items from grandmas, found items, art supplies, or things we made." And her story is more than a self-help-book mantra: After an unstable childhood spent moving between homes, accruing "stuff" seemed a salvation of sorts. "I finally have a real home," she says. "Letting go of the meaningless clutter of knickknacks relieves space for my supplies to become a usable element of decor."

In their few off hours, the couple likes to unwind in their kitchen—which they couldn't help but customize, of course. And in the summertime, they can go down to the local pond for a dip and then a campfire dinner. When asked the key to a happy home, Siosi says, "Function. Maintenance. Music. Rest." Culver's response? "The girl of my dreams plus one dog plus one cat." Siosi replies, "Ha! Yeah, that's what I meant, too."

We love this home's handcrafted elements. They brighten the space with a sense of workmanship and detail.

PREVIOUS SPREAD /
UNIQUE LAYOUT

"Due to the linear confines of our shotgun-style space, it's ever evolving," says Siosi. Here, a collection of plants queues across the living-room wall, while an adjacent wall is painted black to best offset the couple's preferred furniture material: a light ambrosia maple.

OPPOSITE / WORK-LIFE BALANCE

"We live and work together every day and wouldn't have it any other way," says Culver. "We work hard and for long hours, so intermittently we take basketball, ping pong, skateboard, or motorcycle breaks—a little play goes a long way."

ABOVE LEFT / CURATED CLASSIC

While their home is mostly filled with their own creations, a few pieces from design greats had to be included, like this Eames lounge chair. "I'm not a big shopper, but I do care about buying things that last," says Culver.

ABOVE RIGHT / HEY MS. DJ

"The goal for this piece was to accommodate a couple hundred records," said Culver. "Ivy hand-painted the steel base, and I made the shelving from ambrosia maple; and the little table is made from an ambrosia maple slab." According to Culver, "The beauty of being a designer and woodworker is putting together an idea that's just for you. I'm not likely to make another funny little table like this one, but it was fun to make and I'll have it forever."

ABOVE / UTILITARIAN DREAM

This kitchen is a no-fuss workspace, punched up with colorful vintage saucepans, a funky map, whimsical decorative items, and tools confined to a rail above the butcher-block surface. "The most used piece of furniture is our kitchen island," say Culver. "This was a prototype that we made nearly five years ago of our Amagansett Kitchen Island design—our most popular piece to date. Over the years, our island has taken a beating and still looks good as new."

OPPOSITE TOP / TAKING A BREATHER

Ivy Siosi and Audi Culver in their workshop, perched on a pair of stools they made themselves. Live-edge wood slabs lean against the wall in the background.

OPPOSITE BOTTOM / PERFECT PRESENT

"I made the couch for Ivy's 32nd birthday," says Culver. "I'm terrible at surprises, so I told her what the plan was, and we designed it together. I'm a big denim fan, so the upholstery is a nice thick denim and the frame is made from solid ash." That cool item on the wall? A vertical panorama, titled "Ivy," from Culver's MFA thesis show.

OPPOSITE / STAND TALL

A handmade plant stand gives pride of place to one of Culver's passions, her orchids. "When I manage to coax an orchid to thrive, I feel like I've accomplished something," she declares. This room also showcases the home's original wood trim; its good bones attract plenty of attention, thanks to the couple's more minimalist style.

ABOVE / CHILDHOOD KEEPSAKE

"The bed is one of the few pieces we didn't make—it's my childhood bed," shares Culver. They also didn't make this nightstand from scratch, but they still gave it their own personal touch. "This is a piece that we found in a friends' attic," says Culver. "Ivy refinished it and added the drawer pulls." The pair's trademark ledge shelves—so refreshingly simple and pragmatic—provide perches for plants, while abstract artwork lends a sense of intrigue to the understated space. Ultimately, for these two, happiness means having less. For them, visual clutter equals mental clutter.

There's nothing like plants in the bedroom to help you get a good night's rest.

Four Ways to Display a Vignette

1 STACK AND LAYER

An *aah*-worthy vignette gets a boost from dimension and depth, so seek items that introduce various heights (or that can be stacked to fake it!) and that can be layered front to back. Watch your lines: A mix of stabilizing verticals and horizontals, dynamic diagonals, and curvy forms will send the eye on a satisfying trip. If you have a long, uninterrupted surface (hello, credenza), stagger tall and short pieces for a mountain-range effect. Remember to mix up scale, too!

2 CONTAIN IT

A cute option for small collections or one-off items is to contain them, maybe under a cloche, beneath a glass-topped table, or in a cabinet. This style works well for collections of the same kind of item–for instance, displaying perfumes or other products with beautiful packaging atop a vanity, or plants in an artful terrarium. You can also "contain" something by simply grouping it on a tray, a shallow basket, or a textured surface that visually separates it from other items.

So you've identified your objects of affection—items that speak to your experiences and make you happy whenever you see them. Now what? Style them into vignettes of small but pleasing tableaux of items united in colorway but distinct in shape, all arranged artfully. Collections of all sorts lend themselves to being styled into a unique display.

3 GO VERTICAL

Take your keepsakes and collections to new heights by mounting them directly to the wall. (You'll want to make sure that you don't damage the items when hanging them, and remember that some hanging methods are more permanent than others.) The fun part is *how* you arrange them on the wall, of course. Try an overlapping array of items like you see here, go with a more geometric and evenly spaced approach, or even create a meandering line up and across the wall.

4 MAKE A GRAPHIC GRID

Everyone loves things arranged neatly, so experiment with placing your favorite finds in a gridded display. It's great for bringing dissimilar objects together, whether that means highlighting a theme—as with these beachy treasures—or connecting unrelated items that happen to be in a similar colorway and take up more or less the same amount of space. A neat trick? Include one item that breaks the grid in some way for visual interest.

Bohemian Luxury

When it comes to building decor around meaningful objects, look no further than Christina Bryant, co-founder of St. Frank, an interior-design daydream-come-true that stocks high-end textiles and decorative items from a global network of artisans. From living in Rwanda and studying art history at the University of Virginia, to starting her career at New York's MOMA and receiving an MBA from Stanford, Bryant seems uniquely suited to creating a luxury lifestyle brand. Her recent apartment in Pacific Heights was no exception, blending St. Frank's stylish worldliness with fun touches from her personal travel (bonjour, Cap-Eden-Roc towels!) and antique pieces rich in family history. "We describe the St. Frank aesthetic as 'modern bohemian luxury,'" Bryant shares. "I think

my home reflects that point of view, but also my belief that every home should tell the story of its inhabitant. I come from a very traditional family, for example, so you'll see antique hand-me-downs mixed with items from my travels."

"Story" is a word that comes up time and time again with Bryant, and it's refreshing to hear the young retail star rep for authenticity over trends. "Spaces that sing do not feel overly decorated but, rather, specific and meaningful to the person living there," she explains. "That's what distinguishes an interesting home from a hotel lobby."

Bryant's space is surprisingly small—she's packed a globe's worth of inspiration into a studio apartment. Her formula for making it look luxe? "First, investing in a couple of high-impact pieces—like wallpaper or a large piece of art or a beautiful, noticeable light fixture—can really set the tone and anchor the space as someplace special," she says. She also advocates for mixing high and low: "There's no reason a thoughtful piece from CB2 or a flea market find can't sit next to an antique."

As for the curatorial instincts that make her retail venture a success, this self-identified global citizen credits her art-history education and her realization that—beyond prettying up a wall—art can "tell incredibly rich, multifaceted cultural and historical stories." This life-long passion is matched only by her goal of supporting artists and craftspeople in developing regions.

Back at home, all of Bryant's collections, strategic colorways, and enviable print-mixing make for much more than a gallery. "I see my home as a sanctuary—a special space for me to come home to and feel calm and protected," she says. "So I approached it with a focus on taking care of myself, enjoying my personal time, and celebrating my independence." Hear, hear.

Bryant's home is full of inspiring textiles and other finds from her travels abroad.

PREVIOUS SPREAD / THE REST IS HISTORY

The find that sparked the idea for St. Frank was an Indian textile that Bryant bought and framed. It's now on display in her living room alongside indigo pillows from Burkina Faso happily nestled into the armchairs and sofa.

OPPOSITE / TRUE BLUE

"I'm a believer in combining multiple colors and patterns. Don't overthink it, just do it!" Bryant exclaims. In her space, she uses a base of blue and white, then threads in smaller pops of pink, red, purple, and green for contrast and visual variety. She also plays with similar patterns and palettes in different scales, as you see in the wallpaper and tray here.

ABOVE LEFT / MEXICAN MOTIFS

A Día de los Muertos skull in vivid blue grins from its perch on a chicly appointed bar cart.

ABOVE RIGHT / PORTRAIT OF THE ENTREPRENEUR

St. Frank's flagship store is in the Laurel Heights neighborhood of San Francisco—a choice that's hardly incidental. "For me, San Francisco embodies innovation and social progress. Those values are essential to St. Frank, which is why we're named after the city," Bryant relays. "Moreover, I love being surrounded by people who are excited about pushing the envelope and who accept risk taking."

ABOVE / A PATTERN STORY

"This is our Indigo Arrows wallpaper from St. Frank's first wallpaper collection," Bryant shares. "I absolutely love the way it transformed my bedroom. Even though the wallpaper is dark, it actually made the room and the apartment feel bigger. Lying in this blue room at night is the best feeling!" Several pillows on the bed—also from St. Frank—up the oasis factor. The bedroom is possibly Bryant's favorite space: "It's cozy and perched looking out on the world."

OPPOSITE TOP / MAKING ROOM FOR WHAT MATTERS

Even though her home is a studio apartment, Bryant still found a way to include a dining table so she could entertain. Here, three feathery Juju hats line up over the ornately carved dining suite.

OPPOSITE BOTTOM / WANDERLOVE

An etagere of hand-picked books, textiles, and international keepsakes makes for a comprehensive display of Bryant's travels and passions. "My generation is curious about the world, desires and dares to travel off the beaten path and to get to know different people, values authentic pieces with rich stories, demands ethical sourcing, and invests in creating beautiful, storied spaces that are all their own," she says of herself and her clientele. What's her favorite place to visit? "Cuba. I'm totally enthralled with Cuban history and culture. Havana might be my favorite city."

OPPOSITE / MAKING IT NEW AGAIN

"I had two sets of antique chairs from my mom. I love them, but the upholstery was straight out of 1988 — sorry, Mom, I know it was totally chic then!" To get them caught up with contemporary style, Bryant reupholstered both with Rebecca Atwood's Speckled Smoke. "Re-covering furniture can make all the difference in transforming a piece you're tired of into something you suddenly see as spectacular."

ABOVE LEFT / LOVELY LAYERS

Gorgeous glass beads from Ghana work nicely with a plate in a traditional blue-and-white china pattern, while a matchbox carries on a playful skull theme that runs throughout the space.

ABOVE RIGHT / HELLO THERE

An entryway vignette greets visitors with a cheery framed print. When asked how to find the best travel scores, Bryant says: "Find vendors who demonstrate knowledge." Beyond that? "Buy what you love!"

Every detail in this pint-size pad works to enhance it and bring a sense of space and complexity.

Four Ways to Treat Yourself to a Trend

1 TOSS ON A PILLOW OR A THROW

It just doesn't get any easier than a throw pillow, people. Textiles are one of the best ways to play with pattern, color, and texture, because you can swap them out as soon as you're over the trend and they make less of a dent in your budget. They're also easily scalable—if you start by introducing a pillow in one colorway, you can quickly (and perhaps cheaply) upgrade to a rug, a set of curtains, or a tapestry. Try different patterns in different scales to see which suits your space.

2 GET YOUR FIX WITH FIXTURES

Hardware is another quick fix. As we've mentioned before, switching up knobs is one simple yet effective way to bring fresh colors and materials into a space, whether that means au courant jewel-toned ceramics or stylish, bold brass. A switch plate that matches the trim of a room can bring the whole thing full circle, and lighting fixtures and frames for both art and mirrors can also be tied with intention into a color story and then replaced once they feel tired.

Trends are fun (and, let's face it, inescapable), but we all deserve a home that we love for more than a season. Plus, sometimes you really just want the tip of the iceberg rather than the whole shebang. Here, we'll take a look at how you can incorporate an enduring color trend into your home without, say, investing in a big blush sofa. Commitment-phobes, rejoice!

3 DECK THE WALLS

You can take similar small steps with wall color. You don't have to go whole hog and paint an entire room up front. Start by adding an abstract artwork done primarily in the color you want to try out. If it works, audition an accent wall and see how you respond to it. You can also just paint the room trim, or be inspired by Cecilia Casagrande with a wallpaper that celebrates the trend in all its glory. Temporary wallpaper can make a quick change even easier.

4 TOP IT OFF WITH A DECORATIVE OBJECT

It's easy to forget that the objects we love can create a big color impact. (Think about the pretty packaging from your favorite beauty brands—an easy and affordable way to add a pop of color in the bathroom!) Vessels such as serving bowls, vases, candleholders, and trays top the list when it comes to displayables with trend appeal, but don't forget about the more surprising *objets*: crystals and small sculptures, books and journals, and—of course—cut flowers and potted plants.

Bijou Joy

Take one step into the home of Boston-based designer Cecilia Casagrande, and you're likely to hear yourself say, "Just look at those *walls*." Room after room—eleven, to be exact—of bold jewel-tone paint and even bolder wallpaper choices make her space an unforgettable celebration of color and pattern. There's a stately navy-sapphire paint job in the living room and a chic charcoal one in the master bedroom, while a web of teal lines and an explosion of palm fronds bedeck the walls of the dining and rec rooms, respectively. With these wall treatments serving as a cornerstone of inspiration, Casagrande built up and

out, mixing sumptuous fabrics, enviable antiques, and straight-up majestic materials with more modern and family-friendly shapes, hues, and textiles. The result? A regal yet quirky look that's also totally livable.

And Casagrande designed it all herself, which proved to be as easy as a walk in the park—and just as distracting. "It is easier because I can choose what I like, but more difficult because I know of all the amazing choices and I sometimes get overwhelmed," she confesses. When setting out to design the space, Casagrande looked to her time spent across the pond, setting out to evoke the feelings of a London townhouse. "I found lots of dark, moody colors, eclectic lighting, a great mix of modern and antique items—then added lots of plants, warm textures, and funky art," she says.

As for Casagrande's other sources of inspiration, this industry insider does her research. "I fell in love with a photo of a giant blue sofa in a blue room in a *House Beautiful* magazine," says Casagrande, who got the coveted jewel-box look with Farrow & Ball paint in Hague Blue. "I absolutely love my kitchen chandelier, which I also spotted in a magazine, then got to see in New York when furniture shopping for the house. I just had to have one." The gold-and-smoky-glass orbs give the feminine space a welcome dose of avant garde, while more classic gold fixtures and marble surfaces maintain the aristocratic vibe.

There is such a mood of airiness and ease to this kitchen. We want to spend all of our mornings here.

Casagrande describes her home as "modern, luxe, and eclectic." For each room, she picks a focal-point feature—the blue sofa in the living room, a dramatic stove in the kitchen—as a starting point for the rest of the space, layering on for a look that is eccentric yet cohesive, cozy yet sexy. When asked how she maintains a space that is both design driven and family friendly, she says, "I have found that my high-design pieces are significantly better made, and therefore can take my three boys, two cats, and a dog. For example, my kitchen stools have gotten bacon grease all over them, and they still look amazing."

PREVIOUS SPREAD / BLUE ON BLUE

Casagrande was first attracted to the home's high ceilings and massive windows (though she does pine for a little more square footage in the living room). A wingback chair with a matching footrest add a contemporary touch to the otherwise decadent space, with its heavy doses of velvet, gold, wood paneling, and marble. Three scissor wall sconces expand over the large sofa for a bit of practicality, too.

OPPOSITE / LIGHT AND AIRY

Casagrande says having a dream kitchen was nonnegotiable. "The kitchen is the heart of our home," she says. "I love to cook, and my kids love hanging out at the island or banquette. The lighting, hood, wallpaper, and stove—the rest just beautifully highlights those gorgeous elements." The especially lovely breakfast nook is enlivened by a large-scale floral print wallpaper by Ellie Cashman, making the whole space feel like a secret garden. "This bold floral reminds me of a Dutch painting—one you'd sit and relax in front of."

ABOVE LEFT / POSH PATTERN MIXING

Not to be outdone, the basement boasts two-toned floor tile and tropical wallpaper by Timorous Beasties.

ABOVE RIGHT / A GLOBETROTTER'S HAVEN

Casagrande chills in her home office with her Irish red and white setter. The wallpaper here features illustrations of beloved international sites, including the Sydney Opera House, Paris's Arc de Triomphe, and Rio de Janeiro's Christ the Redeemer statue.

OPPOSITE / FINE DINING

Pair these jewel-toned Gubi dining chairs with Kelly Wearstler's iconic wallpaper and you've got yourself one helluva dining room. Saarinen's oval pedestal table in rosewood makes an elegant midcentury gathering spot, while a chandelier of glass globes from Foscarini brings on the lux. Casagrande uses a rug and Roman shades in subdued gray to anchor the room.

ABOVE / NOT SO MELLOW YELLOW

The bedroom—perhaps the quietest, most calming space in the house—gets a fun, high-contrast jolt from Farrow & Ball's dark wall color in Studio Green and chartreuse bedding and wall decor. The pair of School House Electric sconces lends a little glimmer, too.

Casagrande's use of wallpaper and color really adds vibrancy and a modern touch throughout the home.

ABOVE / DIGITAL DAYS

A blue-and-green isometric wallpaper from Cole & Son creates a mesmerizing backdrop in the media room. Not afraid to go full-on modern in this family hot spot, Casagrande opted for a cozy yet chic sectional with a cobalt velvet ottoman.

OPPOSITE / GOLD STANDARD

For a triple dose of glitz, an antique gold mirror above the mantel reflects a gold Sputnik chandelier from Jonathan Adler, while an Impressionistic painting in an ornate gilded frame rests against the bold blue wall. The impressive marble fireplace only adds to the royal ambiance.

THE ART OF THE TABLE

There's no denying the power of the centerpiece. Plus, there's no better place to flex your favorite objects of inspiration—seasonal botanicals, intriguing ceramics, heavenly textiles, glinting glass and silverware—in a display that will literally bring everyone to the table.

VESSELS It's best to pair the container with the bloom: tall and cylindrical for upright blossoms, low and wide for top-heavy beauties. Play with arranging grand displays with height and volume in a single vessel, or trail a low arrangement across the table using multiple small vases. Don't be scared to try an unusual container, like a pitcher.

CUT FLOWERS Mix in more familiar blooms and greenery sprigs with cut botanicals that have an exotic or sculptural feel. Choose foliage that introduces something special: leaves in different shapes, berries, or wispy tendrils. You can also balance out a few superstar blooms with equal-size clumps of smaller, more detailed florals. Try to pace elements at regular intervals, and aim for an arrangement that's around two times the height or width of your chosen vase.

SERVEWARE & TEXTILES
Everything from beautiful wooden spoons and cheese boards to high-shine silverware and textural crockery can be used as decorative elements. Linens lend warmth and opportunities for pattern—try a tablecloth that offsets the flowers and place settings, or that plays right into them. Napkins, place mats, and even decorative ribbon or cut yardage can add welcome variety.

CANDLES Tea lights look lovely in pretty cups or ramekins; they can even float majestically in a dish filled with leaves and petals. Give it a shot! For traditional tapers, try modern candlesticks, or more glam old-fashioned candelabras. Look for ones that reflect light for extra pizazz.

Lush Life

It's not easy being green? Not if you ask Hilton Carter! Born and raised in Baltimore, the filmmaker and plant whisperer currently lives in Hampden, just outside the city center. "It used to be more funky," he remembers. He shares this home with his wife, Fiona, and a veritable jungle's worth of plants. The apartment is in an old cotton mill on the Jones Falls stream that sat abandoned until a real-estate company turned it into apartments in 2013. Carter was smitten with its ionic columns, original hardwood floors, and massive casement windows.

Carter had moved back to Baltimore after a period in New Orleans, which is where his iconic (read: Instagram-famous) plant collection was born. His criteria for the new space was that the "ceiling height had to be perfect," and there needed to be windows to provide ample light for his ever-growing collection of plants and trees.

And "collection" may be putting it mildly. The 1,000-square-foot space is virtually covered in greenery. In total, Carter has about 180 plants in his personal living space alone, and an additional 100 or so in an apartment he keeps for events. Charmingly, he has named most of them—the fiddle fig goes by Treezus, a nod to Kanye's *Yeezus* album—and he works watering time into his weekly schedule so that he doesn't forget. "You have to be self-aware of where your threshold is," he wisely says.

You also have to be aware of how all those plants work together without creating an overgrown mess. Carter's advice? Stagger and layer. "The natural idea is that the thing in the front should be the smaller. In my living room, the fiddle is king, followed by a shorter bird of paradise and an even shorter snake plant." It's also a bit of a puzzle, and he lets the foliage guide him: "Sometimes I'll notice, 'Hm, that monstera shouldn't be next to that pothos—maybe it should be next to a bird of paradise.' I move plants around all the time, trying to find the right mix."

The living room, dining area, and kitchen are downstairs in an open-plan configuration that's conducive to frequent entertaining. Carter wants his visitors to feel at home. "When you come in, you just instantly want to kick off your shoes."

Carter is a big fan of flea markets. "For me, I like furniture that looks worn in but feels now." The space also reflects the personalities of its newlywed inhabitants. His wife Fiona—a former neighbor whom he met when she told him to turn down his music—has different tastes. "She'll tell you I got my way more than she did hers," he laughs, "but she'll also tell you that my taste is better. But it's of course important that our home be a mashup of our previous lives, plus items that we find and fall in love with together."

This home is proof that a personal passion can completely transform a space.

PREVIOUS SPREAD /
A GOOD MOOD

The living room is a dark yet stylish retreat in rich grays and browns, perked up by the vibrant foliage of Carter's plant collection. A lot of people tell him that his space feels more masculine—dark woods, leather, tarnished metals—but to Carter it all feels warm and welcoming. "For the most part it just worked out," he says happily.

OPPOSITE / INCUBATION STATION

Carter has devoted an entire wall in his home's entryway for this handsome and practical display of beakers mounted in blocks (his own woodworking creation), where he starts clippings from larger plants.

ABOVE LEFT / PATINA MAGIC

"I did this crazy painting on the dining space's wall to separate it from the living room," Carter shares. On-trend bucket chairs in playful lime green lend a youthful flair to the round table in a rich wooden finish.

ABOVE RIGHT / YEAR-ROUND
VACATION VIBES

Carter and his wife, Fiona enjoying their verdant window. "Living in New Orleans, everything is so tropical," he recounts. "When I moved back to Baltimore, I just wanted to bring that feeling with me."

OPPOSITE / VINTAGE BIKER STYLE

The motorcycle in the space was Carter's father's at age sixteen. A poster for the cult classic *Buffalo '66* is a nod to one of Carter's other passions and first professional calling: filmmaking.

ABOVE / MIDNIGHT AT THE OASIS

Even the bedroom gets the full-on conservatory treatment. A hammock of ferns above the bed visually stands in for a traditional headboard.

Is there anything more peaceful than a home filled to the brim with plants?

ABOVE LEFT / GREEN WITH ENVY

An easy-to-care-for pothos swirls around this antique gold mirror and classic bar cart setup. To achieve this artistic display, Carter mounted a pot on a wooden shelf and trailed the plant's tendrils around the gilded frame and into an enameled wall sconce.

ABOVE RIGHT / MAKING AN ENTRANCE

Carter credits his home's open feel to its tall ceilings, which help him maximize vertical display options for his plants without the space feeling overcrowded. "The ceilings go from 12 to 25 feet," he shares. "It's small one way and big another way, so it doesn't feel cluttered."

OPPOSITE / CACTI ALERT

Move over, humans: This window seat is all for succulents and cacti. "The plan is to move into a space with a greenhouse someday," Carter half kids, "but I'm not purchasing [plants] for the larger house we'd like to own in the future. I'm purchasing for where we live right now."

CHAPTER FOUR

Putting It All Together

What makes a successful space? According to Morgan Hutchinson, founder of the e-commerce site BURU, the secret to a happy home is "living in it with the people you love most—and always having a good bottle of chilled champagne on hand!"

W hile we agree that bubbly works wonders, the key takeaway here is that the right perspective can make all the difference. The number-one thing that makes for a thoughtful and inspired home might just be as simple as giving yourself room to breathe and making sense of what you already have in place. Play and experimentation are integral to growth (both personally and in your space), and you need to create an environment to allow for that.

As with many things in life, moderation is key. So how do you strike that balance—aesthetically and emotionally—when putting your home together? If you've been following this book in order, you'll likely feel that this is, so to speak, where the rubber hits the road. Once you've taken the time and given yourself permission to really meditate on your space and your relationship to it, and done a deep dive into your inspirations, it's time to roll up your sleeves (probably literally if you're the DIY type), set the mood boards aside, and start making those dreams a reality. It's the moment to go for that bright-green accent wall you've been wanting to try or add small touches of a trend to room – and see what sticks.

Your plans are virtually guaranteed to change and evolve as you go. And that's okay! Sometimes the solution to a seemingly thorny problem takes you in new and exciting directions you might never have imagined. At the end of the day, putting it all together is about accounting for what you have and having the good sense not to worry about what you don't– building a home takes time. Go easy on yourself. In this chapter we'll look at a group of homeowners who tackled this challenge in their own unique ways with beautifully different and defiantly wonderful outcomes. Here are a few tips and tricks to get you started.

START WITH A FLOOR PLAN

This really isn't as intimidating as it sounds, though it's decidedly less fun than daydreaming about a bunch of vacation destinations or art you love. A floor plan is simply a way to get from point A to point B; point A is reading this book on your sofa, point B is your dream home.

Whether you're moving into a new space or reworking an existing one, the steps are the same. First, think about the furniture you'll be keeping, and what you'll want to replace or add. Be thorough—if it's a bedroom, you will need a bed (obviously), but potentially also a dresser or credenza or clothing rack. Will you also want additional seating? A little desk? A makeup table? The same exercise holds true for every room in the house. A little work up front saves you the hassle of dragging things around any more than necessary, as well as the heartbreak of falling in love with a piece and then discovering it won't fit.

PICK FOCAL POINTS

As style icon Diana Vreeland famously said, the eye has to travel—but to what? And why? When you enter a room, it's nice to have your eye drawn progressively from one thing to the next, whether that's from the top down—say, from drapery to finely upholstered seating—or bottom up, from a tufted rug to a piece of colorful art.

You can coordinate certain elements in a room like drapery and upholstery, or create a color palette that uses similar tones for a softer impact. Alternatively, create a more dynamic tableau by inserting a few bold elements into the mix—idiosyncratic pieces can and should work well with less-directional finds, as long as they're to your taste and liking. Just be sure those bold items are working with the flow, rather than derailing it

EXPERIMENT WITH COLOR

Make things matchy-matchy with monochrome to create cohesion, or break up the look up with an accent here or there. Color can be a great way to highlight certain items or areas within a space; alternatively, you can use it to soften the visual impact of a piece or collection of items by dousing them in the same or similar tones. Color is also an easy way to experiment—order sample pots of your favorite shades and see how they look in your home's various spaces, with different lighting options.

GO BIG, THEN GO SMALL

Keep in mind that symmetry is one of the most striking (and simplest) elements in a room; paired-off lamps, chairs, framed works and other decorative objects can really impact a guest's sense of scale. Play with form and volume, and don't forget to consider texture when arranging furniture. Then, carry those same lessons through to more "micro" installations, such as a tabletop or bookshelf.

Restorative Classics

American fashion designer Peter Som is known for his bold runway shows, which are a riot of color, pattern, and statement-making shapes. Som's apartment, on the other hand—a gracious two-bedroom in a prewar building in Manhattan's West Village—is a feat of calming restraint, as well as a masterly mix of unlikely elements. Taking inspiration from old and new, feminine and masculine, and uptown and downtown, Som has pulled together a space that feels uniquely comfortable and deliciously relatable. "My clothing line is where I put my love of bright colors and prints and florals," says the designer. "My apartment is my refuge from all of that. I have a stripe here and there, but it's mostly neutral with pops of color coming from the artwork." His home is a lesson in letting prized possessions sing.

Despite a demanding travel schedule, Som has found himself a resident of the building for almost two decades—multiple lifetimes in New York City years. His home reflects a worldly approach to aesthetics, but acts as a respite from the harried world outside. "The apartment is truly a mix of things I've had for a long time and pieces that I bought after renovating it," says Som. "I love the idea of a sense of ease in dressing—and that extends to how I wanted my apartment to feel: unstudied but still pulled together."

It helps that good taste runs in the family—Som's parents just happened to be architects. Growing up in cosmopolitan San Francisco, they instilled in a young

Som an appreciation for sophisticated silhouettes and pedigreed furniture. "I grew up in a house full of Bauhaus and midcentury furniture, so having modern classics like the Saarinen table reminds me of my childhood." That table anchors Som's dining area, flanked by cane-backed chairs; a two-toned secretary by the German modernist designer Tommi Parzinger hovers nearby. In the adjacent living room a seagrass rug from ABC Carpet & Home serves as a neutral backdrop to a George Smith sofa upholstered in a charcoal fabric by Raoul Textiles; a 20th-century Brutalist coffee table from Elizabeth Bauer Design takes center stage. Contemporary pieces by Mexican artist Jose Dávila and Swedish painter Mia Enell punctuate the walls. "I want comfort and function to be first—but never sacrificing style," says Som. "It's the idea of not trying too hard."

When a neighboring unit came on the market, Som pounced, enlisting local architects Jeffrey Cayle and Ian Colburn to join the two apartments with the hope of improving the space's flow while maintaining its prewar proportions. To maximize space in the cramped kitchen, Som converted a closet in what was once the entry into a pantry with a wine refrigerator. "I was quite obsessed with the kitchen design since I love to cook so much; even with the kitchen doubling in size it was a jigsaw puzzle to get everything I wanted in."

"At the end of the day it feels like a home—comfortable and filled with things that I love and have collected over the years," says Som. "Whether I'm just chilling and watching TV, having a few friends over for dinner, or having a party with 30 people, the space works."

This home really has a modern yet comfortable vibe!

PREVIOUS SPREAD /
APPROACHABLE LIVING
Selections of artworks and cushions add stimulating pops of color within a calm and comfortable home environment.

OPPOSITE / TICKET TO RIDE
A gallery wall and a cherry-red bicycle on a graphic black-and-white rug create a vibrant display in the apartment's entryway.

ABOVE LEFT / BRANCH OUT
In the dining area (which shares square footage with the living space), an arrangement of almond branches picked up from the flower district sits atop a classic white Saarinen table.

ABOVE RIGHT / DESIGNER DETAILS
Som's home is a study in restraint. In a den off the living room, an antique French desk from the 1940s finds a modern counterpoint in Peter Traag's Mummy chair.

OPPOSITE / THE OFFICE

A study of Som's bedroom embraces a more-is-more approach, with a fabric-draped pin board displaying notes and inspiration—some of which may find its way into future collections. "It's the one place I allow a bit of a mess: postcards, mementos, photos—everything!—is here," he says. A rainbow of colored pencils hints at this room's preferred activity: "I love sketching in the study—the light from the window is amazing."

RIGHT / THE MAN HIMSELF

A devotee of classic midcentury styles, Som chose not to work with an interior designer, instead relying on his own experience in the creative industry and his upbringing as the son of architects in San Francisco.

FOLLOWING SPREAD LEFT / FOCAL POINT

The living room's most eye-catching conversation piece: a 20th-century Brutalist coffee table from Elizabeth Bauer Design. Meanwhile, a George Smith sofa upholstered in charcoal fabric by Raoul Textiles fabric is backed by a gallery wall.

FOLLOWING SPREAD RIGHT / MODERN VIBE

Cerused-oak cabinetry and Carrara marble countertops make for a modern kitchen, while open stainless steel shelving and vintage lighting overhead add to the utilitarian vibe and keep with the apartment's historicity.

This kitchen was made for entertaining.

Two Takes on Putting It All Together

ADVICE FROM JILL SINGER & MONICA KHEMSUROV, FOUNDERS OF SIGHT UNSEEN

The founders of design hub Sight Unseen need no introduction in certain circles. They are the de facto cool kids, a discerning duo whose OFFSITE events, held each year during New York Design Week, have become an incubator for the best of the best of the new, the young, and the edgy. Singer and Khemsurov also approach their own living spaces with keen eyes and a similarly strong sense of intent.

KNOW YOURSELF (AND YOUR SPACE)

"My apartment is really small," says Khemsurov with a sigh. "I think I'd have a lot more success with it if it had better bones." She's found her success slowly, over the nine years she's lived there, making it her own incrementally. The space combines her favorite finds with gifts from up-and-coming designers—and a few statement-making showstoppers.

A WORK IN PROGRESS

Singer, on the other hand, describes a put together home as a continual process of accumulation. "Pulling it together for me takes, like, five years. My house is this living, breathing experiment." Singer is constantly getting rid of stuff and seeing what works; what she (and her husband and two young children) can and can't live without. She's not afraid to learn from her mistakes and move on. "I spent $3,000 on a couch," she says, "and I don't even like it anymore." Now, she's saving up to support young, independent designers. "It's important to be omnivorous," she says. "If you just go to one blog you just get that one perspective."

FINDING THE RIGHT MIX

For both women, home is a mix of work and personality that requires blending vintage and mass market finds to truly reflect a personal sensibility. "Rugs and paint are the easiest ways to change up the feel of a room," says Singer, who herself shies away from extensive color explorations as she finds you really need a "vision" to execute color well. "Art, rugs, and plants add the most dimensionality to a room."

ADVICE FROM PIERA GELARDI, REFINERY29 COFOUNDER & EXECUTIVE CREATIVE DIRECTOR

It should come as no surprise that Refinery29's Piera Gelardi has a gorgeous home. What might be surprising is how humble she is about it. "I do think I designed my home, but I didn't have an overall vision," admits Gelardi. "It was much more of an evolution." It's a relatable sentiment that's sure to resonate with many. "Even after five years, it's still a work in progress."

KNOW YOURSELF (AND YOUR SPACE)

Gelardi describes her home as "not a space where I'm looking to reinvent the wheel," citing her approach to her work as the outlet for her more creative energies. Her extensive art collection includes flea market finds as well as one-of-a-kind pieces from close friends. "I have to rein myself in sometimes, because if I kept adding, every wall would be a gallery wall," she admits.

A WORK IN PROGRESS

Painting the apartment was the first order of business for Gelardi and her partner. The space had been cast in an unflattering off-white shade that did little for the artistic temperaments of its new owners. Today, the main dining area is an optic white, the bedroom is a light pink ("I just know I love living in [that color]," says Gelardi), and the living room is drenched in teal. The biggest undertaking they committed to was switching out the kitchen cabinet fronts and the outdated backsplash, which was replaced with a tiled honeycomb pattern—minor improvements that made a big impact.

FINDING THE RIGHT MIX

Placing authenticity over curation has resulted in a lively home that reflects its owners creative impulses without turning them into aesthetic dictators. "Growing up, if I asked [my grandmother] about anything in the house, it had a story," remembers Gelardi. "My home is really rooted in the idea of storytelling. I like being surrounded by things that have meaning to me. I'm not trying to recreate anyone else's space."

NI HAO

Color Theory

Morgan Hutchinson's Salt Lake City home is a master class in color coordination. The founder of ecommerce fashion site BURU, Hutchinson proudly describes her home as a "box of Skittles," and it's not hard to see why: every room is deeply saturated in vibrant tones that most would shy away from. How does Hutchinson make it work?

The 1920s Federal Heights Tudor-style home needed to be completely renovated to suit Hutchinson's style. Working with Atlanta-based designer Meredith McBrearty, Hutchinson set about creating a space that felt casual and contemporary while still respecting the property's heritage. "Pretty much every nook and cranny was touched," she remembers. "In some cases, it was just paint and refinishing since the house was really dark before; we just tried to brighten all the spaces—painting all the dark trims a bright and glossy white."

But painting, while it gave the Hutchinsons a new canvas to work with, didn't fix some of the structural issues with the home. "As is the case with many homes built in this era, it was lacking a proper master suite," remembers Hutchinson. "We moved a staircase on the second floor and a few walls to create a proper master bathroom and closet, as well as a Jack and Jill bathroom to service the other two bedrooms on the second level. The kitchen also got a major overhaul."

A formal living and dining room flank the entry, with matching arched case openings. Original crown moldings and lead-trimmed windows add even more period specificity. "Growing up in the south, with a mother who always had the dining room table fully set with sterling and china—you know, 'just in case,'—it was important for me to have a formal dining and living room. In no way I am trying to insinuate that we were 'fancy' people. I just come from a line of women who like to entertain!"

The kitchen formed around the white La Cornué range with brass knobs as it was "the only option" for Hutchinson. "We had a custom brass hood made and mounted it on a solid slab of honed Calacatta Gold marble—the same marble that we used for the countertops, island and waterfall. To finish out the space and add some warmth we chose a gorgeous, hand-painted silk Porter Teleo fabric in pink and orange, then added a hot pink banquette seat and throw pillows made of vintage Hermès scarves."

In the living room, the ceiling is papered in Kelly Wearstler's Channels in black and white to eye-catching effect, mediated by ombre draperies, an inspired DIY project created by sewing together wide strips of solid-colored silk. "Meredith got on board immediately, and I think the finished product is really fun and different than anything I've seen before." It's that gung-ho approach—and meticulous follow-through—that makes the Hutchinson's family home feel so colorfully considered. "On top of loving the house and its character, we really love the neighborhood. It's full of old homes, all with their own aesthetic. Nothing cookie cutter about it."

We love that this home really goes there. Its use of patterns and statement items is so exciting.

PREVIOUS SPREAD /
COLOR AND TEXTURE

The wall-papered ceiling is an unexpected touch. "I fell in love with it instantly," says Hutchinson. "I love that it gave the room some texture without taking away from the other color used throughout the space."

OPPOSITE / SUCH A DOLL

The main focal point in the dining room is the glass and brass ram's-head dining table, but Hutchinson's favorite piece in the room is the custom portrait of Barbie and Ken that she commissioned from photographer David Parise for her husband's birthday (they met at Bemelmans's Bar in New York's Carlyle Hotel).

ABOVE LEFT / NO SPACE WSTED

In a house this old and of this style, rooflines and windows present big challenges. In a stroke of genius, McBrearty found a way to turn a completely wasted hallway and tiny laundry room into the perfect dual vanity bathroom for a growing family.

ABOVE RIGHT /
AN ARTISTIC APPROACH

"For us, art is a way to make memories. Rather than pick pieces from specific artists, we often buy them when we are traveling to commemorate a special trip or give them to each other for holidays—anniversaries and birthdays—to mark the date.

*Rainbow curtains and
pillows? Yes, please!*

OPPOSITE / TASTE THE RAINBOW

Hutchinson actually majored in interior design in college although, as she says, "the fashion bug seemed to bite quickly!" Working with a trusted designer helped make her quirky, colorful dreams come true.

ABOVE / LIVE HAPPY

"Color makes me happy. I would like to think it also makes my family and guests happy when they are in the space. My dream word for others to describe our house would be just that—happy!"

ABOVE LEFT / SITTING PRETTY

Hutchinson runs her very successful fashion business out of the house, and the whole family loves to gather in the kitchen and its adjacent sitting room. With its pops of pink, the bright, clean space just feels like home.

ABOVE RIGHT / THINK PINK

The hand-painted Porter Teleo roman shades really bring a sense of warmth to the room and the art creates a very personal feel. "In a way," Hutchinson says, "this room is like sitting in a big memory box. It may not be the most unique space of the house, but it's certainly where we migrate as a family. The space kind of does it all—plus it connects to the backyard through French doors so we have a nice indoor-outdoor thing going on."

OPPOSITE / A POP OF FUCHSIA

The inspiration for her daughter's room started with this chartreuse chinoisserie wallpaper that Hutchinson discovered while flipping through wallpaper books at Alice Lane Home. Hutchinson recalls that Olive had made it pretty clear that she also wanted some pink in the room, "So I gave her a choice of four different pink silks for her window treatments. Like mother like daughter I suppose—she chose the boldest fuchsia in the bunch!"

Four Ways to Play with Color & Pattern

1 MONOCHROMATIC

Monochrome doesn't have to mean meh. Using one cohesive hue can help tie wildly disparate design elements of a room together, and create visual continuity between otherwise seemingly random objects and decorative touches. Decide on your "base tone" and embellish the color story from there. Here, for example, we started with a rich, dark blue. Building out from that base color opens up a world of deeper indigos, paler sky tones, and every hue in between.

2 ANALOGOUS

Analogous color schemes are kind of like monochrome on steroids. The idea is to incorporate colors that sit next to each other on the color wheel to create visual cohesion with a little extra kick. Analogous colors match well and tend to yield combos that feel natural for the simple reason that they're often found in nature. In the example above, we drew on three wedges of the color-wheel pie—true greens and their neighbors, the yellow-greens and the blue-greens.

With a world of colors at your fingertips, how on earth does anyone make the right choices? The key is to mix a little bit of science with a lot of style. The science comes in the form of that design essential, the color wheel. We give some mix-and-match ideas here to get you started coloring your world. Just remember, your personal taste should always carry the day.

3 COMPLEMENTARY

If you've expertly arranged your monochrome moment, and it just feels like it's missing a certain something, complementary colors may be the little shot of spice you need to set off your primary scheme. To find any shade's complementary hue, look to the opposite side of your color wheel. For our indigo room, a few key objects in rusty orange tones will make those blue pieces sing. To bring a little pop to your lush green color scheme, try a cushion or statement vase in a blush tone.

4 WILD CARD

You know how they say that you need to understand the rules in order to break them? Now's your chance! That lovely indigo scheme we started with? Once you've played with analogous colors (a little teal here, a splash of purple there) and carefully coordinated your complementary pieces, go ahead and throw caution out the window. Mix in hues that intimidate and bold patterns that verge on clashing. If you love the results, who cares what the rulebook says?

Dream Weaver

Aelfie Oudghiri's passion for textiles started in childhood. "My mom had a great textile collection. I grew up on a big Kerman rug," she recalls. "That was my first childhood encounter, my first experience with the importance and longevity of textiles." She didn't wait long to start her own collection. "I was 17 or 18 and had just gotten my first credit card, which had a $2,000 limit. That's when I bought my first rug. My mom was shocked; she thought it was pretty irresponsible. But I still have it—I'm looking at it right now, in fact. It's a great rug."

The next step in her journey happened while Aelfie was still a student at Columbia University. "My stepmother's family friend had been a really successful carpet dealer," she explains. "I went out to her house in Long Island and had an old-school tea with her, and she took me to her basement, where she had a ton of crazy textiles." And then she spoke the life-changing sentence, "I just want to get rid of my collection." Aelfie took all her tribal textiles, put them into suitcases, and brought them to her student housing at Columbia. "That's how I got started," she recalls, "selling them on eBay and to random anthropology students."

When she graduated, her apartment was still filled with rugs—piles and piles of rugs. "I was seriously trying to get a job," she says, "I was stressed, doing odd jobs and putting flyers out in the neighborhood. I made an Etsy page and posted on Craigslist. My rug

showroom in Brooklyn was also my apartment." She started getting word-of-mouth business from wealthy entrepreneurs who would tell their friends, "You have to go to this crazy Bushwick loft."

In the spring of 2012, she started designing carpets. "I'd gotten a really good sense of what people were looking for in the years I'd been selling antique and vintage rugs. I knew there was a market for new designs. I hadn't really seen anything fun and innovative happening. I'd been looking at pictures in the library and doodling; I started asking if anyone knew any weavers." Then, in December 2012, *New York* magazine ran a piece on her showroom "and it just took off from there."

All of Aelfie's production takes place in Northern India's Uttar Pradesh region. "I wanted to do something that made sense for the area, and they've been making dhurries for centuries," she explains. As for her modern design inspirations? "A huge part of it came from being in Bushwick—all the street art, fashion, and nightlife there was really inspiring. I also went to the Metropolitan Museum, which has a great Islamic art wing." She recalls looking at a big, beautiful kilim woven by Uzbeki people, and saying to herself, "Man, I wish I had this in black and white."

Not only that, "I wanted a pink rug, I wanted to do more yellow and blue. And black. The new rugs are definitely a reaction to the antique and vintage varieties; I wanted to address the person who couldn't find the perfect vintage rug."

She still finds inspiration in her very first purchase. "It almost looks as if it were miswoven," she says. "It has a really unusual look to it while still being within the language of floral Turkish carpets." She spent eight hours negotiating with the dealer. "I kept saying, 'It looks like they messed up—can't you do something for me?' And he said, 'There's no such thing as mistakes in carpets.'" And I just thought that was so great—that was how they're supposed to be.

PREVIOUS SPREAD /
DYED IN THE WOOL

"I was thinking, 'Man, I wish I had a sheepskin that looked as if it had been painted in watercolors,'" says Aelfie. "Then I met this girl who was a professional dyer at an event in Bushwick." The result: her Cumulus collection.

OPPOSITE / LOVE OBJECT

Aelfie first saw this chair, with its distinctive Central Asian suzani fabric, while she was still a student. She coveted it from afar, and bought it soon after graduation.

ABOVE LEFT / FORTUITOUS FIND

Aelfie started out selling her rugs on Craigslist, where she also found one-of-a-kind treasures, like this red dresser.

ABOVE RIGHT / GOING MOBILE

This eye-catching geometric mobile came from a seller on Etsy.

ABOVE LEFT / PILLOW TALK

A pink sofa from CB2 is the dainty base for strong accents, including the designer's playful "Saelfie" pillow.

ABOVE RIGHT /
FAMILY RESEMBLANCE

Chilling on the couch with her eight-month-old daughter Mirah, domestic bliss has never looked so vibrant.

OPPOSITE / SHOW AND TELL

Aelfie's Greenpoint studio feels like a natural extension of her living space, providing continuity and a unified aesthetic—with a little more breathing room than that first showroom, aka her Brooklyn apartment.

OPPOSITE / BABY STEPS
In Mirah's room, the daybed is covered with a Moroccan
textile that was a present from Oudghiri's husband, Hicham.

ABOVE / SWEET DREAMS
A wall hanging inspired by a Josef Albers painting is
displayed above a bed dressed in samples from Oudghiri's
line. The beaded Yoruba chair at right is from Nigeria.

*We're big fans of all the
textures in this bold home.*

Four Ways to Play with Material & Texture

1 GLAM

The luxe life is achievable no matter what your budget looks like. Velvets, silks, rich brocades and embroideries pack a punch in doses small and large. If you can't splurge on a velvet sofa, you can glam up your space with pillows, wall hangings, and accent pieces in rich jewel tones and lush fabrics. Layer them gratuitously and with abandon. Apply the same principle to luxury materials like marble, mahogany, and fine leathers. A little touch goes a long way.

2 BOHEMIAN

The bohemian aesthetic is all about effortless ease and funky hand-crafted authenticity. Look for wood furniture with a craft feel, like woven and rattan seating and tables, or patinaed vintage pieces with a hand-hewn look. A kilim or other bright rug can bring in multiple colors in one pattern but works equally well when overdyed. Search flea markets and second-hand stores for mercury glass vases or jewel-toned glassware that's easy to mix and match.

Adding visual interest to your space can come from a variety of items and textures, whether layering faux furs on a sofa, devoting wall space to textile art, or deciding on a glaze for dinnerware. Everyone has their own aesthetic; these styles here can help give you an idea of what speaks to yours most clearly—and even perhaps add something new and unexpected!

3 FUTURISTIC MINIMALISM

Embrace a modern take on 1960s space-age staples including chrome accents, molded plywood, acrylic fixtures, and vinyl surfaces—no lava lamp or go-go boots required. In fact, all of these retro staples feel fresh again, thanks in large part to young designers working to remake them in a modern vernacular. Use these elements sparingly to create a cohesive, compelling space that references design's past while staying true to its future

4 SCANDI COZY

The new Nordic minimalism isn't about austerity; in fact, this iteration of the Scandinavian aesthetic is indulgently warm and welcoming. Get the look by mixing ceramic, woolen wovens and natural birchwood. Layer textiles over your sofa and seating to invite repose and invest in light woods that look as good bare as they do laden with a night's meal. Create tableaus with hand-hewn ceramic vessels, jars, and dishware—everything from candle holders to salt cellars.

Grand Designs

Designer and House of Honey owner Tamara Kaye-Honey does not shy away from the grandiose. Her Southern California home is full of epic mishes and mashes, colorful juxtapositions and unexpected moments that draw the eye upward, outward and all over. "I think of our house as a sort of testing lab where I can try out new ideas and vignettes," says Kaye-Honey. "I often sell pieces to clients or swap out furniture and accessories from the shop. It's not uncommon for [my husband and children] to come home after an outing at the playground to find many things moved—or even replaced."

The designer installed a European-style standing-seam metal roof and timber detailing to the home's exterior; during the second phase of renovations, the Honeys added a pool, guest house, and cabana to the grounds. "It's crucial for me to have easy access to the outdoors, as it is definitely a big part of our living space," she says. "We spend most days with the doors open and the kids running to and from the yard."

In the living area, Kaye-Honey offset the heaviness of the original Australian gum wood crown molding and Batchelder fireplace with Italian Murano glass sconces and a vintage brass C. Jeré sculpture over the fireplace. "I worked for a company that imported Danish modern years ago in New York City, and I have not been able to part with any of the pieces," says Kaye-Honey.

PREVIOUS SPREAD /
FULL STEAM AHEAD
A custom steam shower outfitted with brass
fixtures by Waterworks rests in one of the
home's existing gables. Metallic touches are
the only moments of color in the dominantly
white bathroom.

ABOVE / COLLECTOR'S ITEM
A broad selection of Kaye-Honey's vast
collection of midcentury works creates a
functional but fanciful aesthetic.

OPPOSITE / OPEN DOOR POLICY
Taking a moment to enjoy the home's indoor-
outdoor flow, Kaye-Honey prefers to open her
house to its outdoor environs—a space that is
as much a part of the home as its interior.

The Milo Baughman table in the dining room, flanked by Eero Saarinen Tulip chairs, was purchased on Craigslist from an elderly artist who'd used it in her studio for nearly 30 years. "It was covered in paint splatters when it arrived, but a bit of Goof Off and it looks brand-new," says Kaye-Honey. "I try to combine high- and low-end pieces and materials, both new and vintage, in unexpected ways to create fresh yet timeless spaces for myself and my clients."

Upstairs, a trompe l'oeil wallpaper by Deborah Bowness transforms a den into a gracious reading nook. "I wanted that space to be my library, but the engineer said the house could not take the load [of a wall full of shelving]," says Kaye-Honey. "The wallpaper does the trick!"

The home's original attic was converted into a master suite—as well as an office, den, and media room—in the footprint of the house's dormers and gables. One of the most jaw-dropping features has to be the master bath's freestanding Victoria + Albert Napoli tub overlooking a view onto fruit and avocado trees. The tub filler is Henry by Waterworks in unlacquered brass. "It's starting to patina, and I love the juxtaposition of the modern tub with the old-looking fittings," says Kaye-Honey. A custom steam shower outfitted with brass fixtures by Waterworks rests in one of the home's existing gables.

If it sounds like almost too much, you'd be right. This family home walks right up to that line—glamorous, but not gauche, golden, not gaudy—and does it with panache. After all, this isn't a regular home: it's the House of Honey.

Every home needs a statement art piece!

This home really feels high-design, yet lived in—a tricky balance to pull off.

THE ART OF THE FLOOR PLAN

The floorplan is a simple and effective tool that can make a huge difference in the way you put a room together. And, for our purposes, it doesn't have to be accurate to the smallest measurement. You can rough one up by hand, on a tablet, even in Microsoft Excel. The goal is simple: knowing what you have and how to make it work together, harmoniously.

CONSIDER SPACING Planning where to place tables, seating, and particularly cabinets and storage items with hinged doors will help you avoid any headaches down the line. The last thing you want is a "perfect" credenza that opens directly into your sofa.

MEASURE FOOTPRINTS

Measuring the footprint of each piece of furniture you'd like to have in a room is an important first step. Note the height as well so that you'll know which pieces will fit under a window. Now you'll be able to decide which of your furniture to keep and what needs to go.

BE INTENTIONAL WITH GROUPINGS

While some traditional arrangements might work in your space—a sofa often faces a coffee table, often across from two arm chairs with a side table in between for drinks—it's important to deconstruct what's typically done and find the way it applies to your lifestyle and space constraints.

GET ORIENTED
Use your phone's compass to determine which parts of your room face north, south, east, and west. Keep in mind where the sun comes in and at what times so that you can orient your furniture, TV, and plants accordingly.

DEMARCATE WITH TEXTILES & ART
Area rugs can help to break up a room visually by demarcating certain spaces for lounging, dining or simply passing through. Place dark or patterned rugs in areas where there's heavy foot traffic to cut down on cleaning costs. Art placement is another way to break up a room visually, drawing the eye to different elevations within a space or to a specific focal point at one end of the room or the other.

BE AWARE OF INCONSISTENCIES
If your space has wonky measurements or strange protrusions, see if you can find a way to accommodate them in your plan. Use a ruler or protractor to create straight lines and right angles. If not, simply make a note that, for instance, the back wall is slightly shorter on the right-hand side than the left. These small variances generally won't matter too much.

The Bare Essentials

Whittling down your domain is no easy feat. Even if, like husband-and wife duo Hrishikesh Hirway and Lindsey Lund Mortensen, you're a pair of self-proclaimed minimalists who share an artistic vision and a passion for design. They made the jump from renting to searching for the perfect home when, as they say, "Our work life kept overtaking our living space and we knew it was time to try and find a larger space to house our growing dreams and ambitions" while staying true to their streamlined design sense. They found all that and more in LA's Eagle Rock neighborhood where designers Brian and Kathrin Smirke had renovated a number of older homes (you might recognize them from their Insta-famous renovation project, Dome In the Desert.)

"We saw the house and immediately loved it," they recall, "because of the amount of natural light and the backyard which was perfect for intimate dinner parties."

They decided that they both have to be in agreement and passionate about anything that they bring into the home—luckily their aesthetic vision has a lot of overlap. "We've found that sticking to a very simple and neutral palette has made things easier as well as trying to abide by a principle that everything and every object in our home, whether functional or decorative, has to individually be a piece that we love and makes us happy."

They cite their design icons as Isamu Noguchi, Axel Vervoordt, Le Corbusier, and George Nakashima, yet have found ways to bring that feel to the home without breaking the bank.

"There are two things that we've splurged on," says Lindsey, "and each one was a gift for the other person! On the day we got married, I gave Hrishi a beautiful Arthur Ou photograph that I had specially framed. It was something that we had both admired for awhile and I also loved that the artist was someone that Hrishikesh had as a TA in his photo class while in college. The other item is a Phil Chang print that Hrishikesh gave me as a birthday present."

One-of-a-kind furnishings include a treasured kitchen table made as a wedding present from a dear friend, and a TV console passed down from Lindsey's aunt. That piece originally belonged to Lund's grandmother, who purchased it in the '60s. "We were thrilled to learn that the console has built in speakers (that still worked!) and a turntable with the original owners manual."

Some people might be surprised how low-budget the home's other furniture is. "A lot of the things in our home have come from either IKEA, Target, or Craigslist. With the IKEA pieces, we've just been extremely picky and selective and often modify the pieces to make it seem less 'Ikea-ish'. For example, our bed frame and side table both came from Ikea. They're actually the cheapest pieces you can get from there in terms of bedroom furniture, but they're also the only pieces that are solid wood. Which was important to us. They come as a raw color which made it perfect to stain them a walnut color to match the rest of the wood color in our home."

Remember to give the items in your home space to breathe (and show off).

PREVIOUS SPREAD / LIGHT AND EASY

What's the couple's design philosophy? "We aim to keep things simple and natural by limiting our palette and materials and hopefully create a home that has a calm and inviting atmosphere but that also feels cozy."

OPPOSITE / JUST THE BASICS

This bookcase is one of the home's few, precious built-ins. Storage is a constant struggle, so to keep things in an uncluttered equilibrium, they've had to practice restraint and mindfulness about possessions, including a 'one in, one out' approach to anything that they decide to bring into their home.

ABOVE LEFT / PICTURE PERFECT

This Arthur Ou print has pride of place in the serene, airy bedroom. "I love it because it's simultaneously both a photo and a painting," confesses Lindsey, "because of the artist's technique of painting ink jet printer ink on ink jet paper."

ABOVE RIGHT / WORKING TOGETHER

Lindsey is a fashion designer with an art background; Hrishi a musician and podcaster whose background includes photography and graphic design. These influences apply to all the work that they do, regardless of the medium.

OPPOSITE / FOUND OBJECTS
Minimalist decor pieces, sourced from local L.A. boutiques like Poketo, Lawson-Fenning, and Garde, sit comfortably alongside fortuitous finds from Craigslist, local flea markets, and even IKEA.

ABOVE / SHINE A LIGHT
The simplistic kitchen design foregrounds this Brendan Ravenhill pendant light. "We're such huge fans of Brendan's," they explain, "and were so excited when we were able to install one of his pieces in our home."

ABOVE / THE SMALLEST DETAIL

"Hrishi can't stand when lighting has different color temperatures," Lindsey notes, "so wherever we live, he always makes sure to synchronize the lighting."

OPPOSITE / A PERFECT BALANCE

Even the smallest items in the home are carefully curated, pared down and simplified. Here, an Isamu Noguchi lantern anchors an organic trio of items.

Carefully curated vignettes really make this home feel personal.

CHAPTER FIVE

Maintaining Your Truth

As the saying goes, change is the only constant. And, as your life shifts and leads you down different paths, your home should subsequently evolve with it. It's rarely an easy ask, but meeting the challenge can be well worth it.

M aybe you've taken a look around and realized that your gallery wall of flea-market art or collection of milk-glass vases don't set off a spark in the same way they used to. Or perhaps you've taken up a new hobby or even moved in with someone and the way you function in your space is radically different? Who's to say why or what will alter your presence and perspective in your home, but once you find yourself feeling uninspired or craving change—it's time to take action.

Reflecting on your growing values, realities, and tastes is an exploratory exercise that will lead you in the right direction to truly being present within your abode. It's rarely easy, but meeting the challenge can be well worth it.

In this chapter we'll break it all down—how to approach your home as something that's living and breathing and ready to be the backdrop for some of life's most memorable experiences. What does it look like to be in dialogue with your home? How do you create an ongoing relationship with your space and the things that you choose to bring into it?

Change can come in many forms. For Desanka Fasiska of Lux Eros, a new baby helped her look at her home with fresh eyes. For activist and author Jodie Patterson, divorce moved her into a new space but her focus on personal growth and family continued to amplify.

Change isn't always caused by a major life event—sometimes it's precipitated by quiet moments of introspection. Having an "ah-ha" during yoga is just as valid a reason for change as an expanding family or new job. It's important to reflect on who needs what from you and think about how you're going to give it to them, but it's also vital to ask: What do you need from yourself? What does an ideal space look like that serves those needs? And what does it look like to be in constant conversation with *your* home? Let's find out.

LISTEN & REFLECT

You know what they say—when life gives you lemons, make lemonade. "They" weren't necessarily talking about design decisions, but where there's a will there's a way. We truly believe that everything in your home takes up space not just IRL but in your energy and how you face the world. So, when incorporating a new element into your home life, it's important to reflect on how it may alter the ebb and flow of your living situation. No need to do anything drastic here—at this point just listen and let anything that wants to bubble up come to you.

RECLAIM

Take time to re-contextualize a space. You are the one in charge of your destiny, but also your living room. Maintaining your truth in a space that feels like it doesn't serve your needs is hard. Take a minute to think about how you want to function, and more importantly, feel in it—and examine how whatever you're adding (or subtracting) will shift the space. If you're losing an element in a space, be it a person who's headed off to college or a large piece of furniture that is hard to part with, you'll want to make a plan for coping with that. Be realistic about it and the process. Reclaiming a space involves a good amount of self-reflection—don't be afraid to feel it.

REINVENT & RECONSIDER

If major renovations aren't in the budget, ask yourself if they're even really necessary. Consider how you really use the space and what kinds of shifts might be necessary to make it work for you. It doesn't necessarily mean you need to go out and add new furniture or go all Marie Kondo on every corner. Perhaps there are small shifts based on your growing interests or life changes—like adding more light, sprucing things up with an accent wall, or creating a quiet corner for where you unwind after work.

RELOCATE

It can be admittedly hard to maintain your truth during a move. Hopefully such a big life change is spurred on by something positive, but even a move that feels like a necessary evil can become an opportunity for growth and evolution. Use this opportunity to thoroughly assess what you're bringing into your space. Now is the time to chuck anything that isn't helping foster the person or energy you reclaimed. Let it go, and move onwards and upwards.

Two Takes on Maintaining Your Truth

ADVICE FROM LATHAM THOMAS, DOULA & FOUNDER OF MAMAGLOW

Latham Thomas describes her personal style at home as eclectic, indulging elements of mid-century modernism and bohemian chic in equal measure, with an eye for bold punches of color and lots of light. Her design choices reflect the importance of community in her life, and she also emphasizes the impact of a home's energy. "Every time we enter a space, we enter a portal—a portal into a new way of thinking or being, a new experience," she says.

THE IMPORTANCE OF ENERGY

"Whether you're choosing a sofa or a floral arrangement, you're going to be selecting for what you think is going to make people feel comfortable and appreciated," says Thomas. To carry that feeling of warmth and welcome throughout her space, Thomas, a doula and the founder of Mama Glow, a maternity lifestyle brand, focuses on energy. "I always think first about how I want to feel," she says.

FORM FOLLOWS FEELING

In her own home, a townhouse in Williamsburg, Brooklyn, she makes people her top priority. Walls were taken down to open up the space and carry through a sense of communal living. "I love entertaining. I think it's because when I grew up there were so many family gatherings centered around food and holidays," says Thomas, who believes in a set table at all times. "it shows that there's plenitude here, and that we're ready to serve you. Even if it's just girlfriends gathering to watch the season finale of a show, I take that as an opportunity to pour love into the moment and create ritual around spaces."

MINDFULNESS IN ALL THINGS

The loft-like space facilitates connections between Thomas and her close-knit family, as well as guests and clients, who use the garden level as a women's center complete with a sanctuary and event space. The women who come bring a certain energy as well. "My intention for what I wanted it to be became a directive in how to design it," says Thomas, who outfitted the interior in a watery rose hue and supplied velvet settees to create a "cozy, open" feeling. "I feel like we should always be designing for beauty."

ADVICE FROM JESSICA LANYADOO, ASTROLOGER & PSYCHIC MEDIUM

Jessica Lanyadoo is an astrologer by trade and a self-professed obsessive when it comes to "the energetics of spaces." "After doing a clearing of a space I will often use rosewater to bring in more heart energy," says Lanyadoo, who also uses tools like sage and palo santo to facilitate inner peace. She pays close attention to sensory details, such as "being really intentional about where I put lamps and the quality of light that I use."

THE IMPORTANCE OF ENERGY

Lanyadoo is more concerned with the way her space feels than the way it looks. She collects vintage wood furniture because it has good energy, and because thrifting and shopping vintage is a great way to lessen the environmental impact of materialism. "Too many things that you're not connected to can make your home feel dull," says Lanyadoo. "I'm a really big fan of touching my stuff to create and impart good energy." She adds, "When you're dreaming of a home, you're dreaming of a consciousness," noting that she sometimes purposefully moves elements around to stimulate growth and change.

FORM FOLLOWS FEELING

"My approach to physical space is function and feeling," she says. "I'm an energy person." That means Lanyadoo is very intentional about how she uses that space, viewing the home as an extension of the self rather than a static space. Her myriad collections inform that sense of self and include cork lamps and furniture, ceramics and crystals, plants and planters—and lots of books. ("I love their function and the way they look.")

MINDFULNESS IN ALL THINGS

To keep things personal she collects the art of her friends, mixed together as she pleases. A major focus for Lanyadoo, who works from home, is setting boundaries and making aesthetic choices to support them. "I set my energy when I sit down to work at my dining-room table. I light a candle—fire means energy—and then I focus on an activity; when I blow out the candle, that activity is done," she says. "Being consistently clear about what you're using a space for is important."

The A List

Lux Eros ceramics founder Desanka Fasiska's Hollywood Hills A-frame home is every bit as unique and cool as her artwork. The home, built from a Sears kit in 1963, appealed to Fasiska's nostalgic side—evoking the A-frame getaway her father had built long ago in West Virginia. "I think my happiest family memories were in that lake house, so when I saw this house I knew it was supposed to be mine. It took a while, as it was actually in escrow to another buyer when I found it. But, one thing led to another and it came back to me!"

Fasiska dubbed her new home the Lux Lodge, and opened it up to events and gatherings for local artists. Having worked in fashion design for over a decade before starting her ceramics business, she has a confident and seemingly effortless style, which she describes as "Biba meets Big Sur." "It's very California-earthy but with a '70s glam twist," she says. Those influences express themselves in the home's neutral-toned furniture and decorative accessories, arranged throughout to complement the home's cabin aesthetic. "I'm just not good with bright and loud," says Fasiska. "I can only feel sane in an earthy home."

That blissful sanity was put to the test in the best possible way, by the introduction of a new family member, baby Rocky, who arrived in 2017. Fasiska recalls that she wanted the baby's room to be cute and cozy, even though, because of the home's small size, that space ended up being in the foyer. "The space ending up lending itself perfectly to being the nursery," she says.

While the process of making this dream home her own required some expert help due to the home's tricky proportions and slanted walls, setting up the nursery was highly personal. Fasiska followed her instinct and inspiration to "not only bring in cute animal details but also more sophisticated design elements," like hanging a vintage mirror above a cute elephant-themed dresser from Pottery Barn.

Once Rocky is little older, Fasiska looks forward to resuming hosting workshops, events, shoots, and more. "I love creating a space for people who don't know each other to come together and feel connected through a mutual love of exploring their creativity," she says. Striking that balance as a mom is hard, but can be done—as Fasiska's home demonstrates in the choices she's made throughout.

The garden is one of the property's most impressive features, and all the more so when you find out that Fasiska IKEA-hacked it herself. "I made the sitting area using pallets and the cheap IKEA mattresses that I just Scotch-Guarded and covered with fitted sheets. I have to replace the sheets every so often, but it's way cheaper than buying outdoor furniture," she says.

For the bathroom, a claw-foot tub fit perfectly into a big A-frame window. "That window was just sitting in the bedroom as empty space," she recalls. "The architect I worked with had the idea to put the bathroom there, and we both decided it would be even more amazing if it was just open in the bedroom as a design feature."

Fasiska's personality is also reflected in the ceramics that fill the house. "The kitchen has all my studio reject plates, bowls, and vases," she laughs. "[But] I sometimes will bring up some of the nice stuff I make for actual paying customers and use them in my home, too."

This home oozes lightness and serene vibes.

PREVIOUS SPREAD /
A LITTLE EXTRA

Fasiska considers herself a minimalist but doesn't mind a little "extra" here and there. Here, her neutral-toned dining area gets a hint of muted color from a rug that she swiped from her mother, who originally purchased it in Santa Fe, New Mexico.

OPPOSITE PAGE / NEUTRAL ZONE

Because this house is basically all wood, she notes that keeping the natural feel meant mixing an interesting array of natural textures and materials.

ABOVE LEFT / LIGHT AND AIRY

Greenery, dried grasses, and natural wood tones throughout the light-filled home make the boundary between indoors and outdoors delightfully blurred. In fact, she's hoping to add a greenhouse in the not-too-distant future.

ABOVE RIGHT / PERFECTLY PLATED

Much like the home itself, Lux Eros ceramics effortlessly blend natural, earthy tones with on-trend colors and embellishments inspired by the artist's background in fashion design.

ABOVE LEFT / ROOM FOR ONE MORE

The extra room that used to be a combination foyer/
sunroom/mudroom is now Rocky's nursery. Luckily,
the home's layout allows guests to be easily redirected
to the back door.

ABOVE RIGHT / CUTE AND COZY

When it came to nursery decor, Fasiska opted not
to follow a strict design theme. "I thought I would do
something around animals," she says, "so I chose a
safari inspiration."

OPPOSITE / CRIB NOTES

For the crib skirt, "I bought a bunch of African mud
cloths at the flea market and made it myself by just
draping under the crib. I used two different motifs to
add more texture," she says.

NEXT SPREAD / LEFT
BATHING BEAUTY

The A-frame design "lent itself to some really cool
features that I took advantage of, like putting the claw-
foot tub in the window and having it exposed to the rest
of the bedroom," she says. "The trickiest thing though is
that you can't hang art on the walls, but I sort of like an
uncluttered space anyway so it works for me."

NEXT SPREAD / RIGHT
GARDEN PARTY

"I made the totems in the little totem garden in my
ceramic studio," she says. "I do a lot of puttering
around the garden doing little DIY and planting
projects, so things are always changing out there."

Four Ways to Mix Different Styles

1 GLAM + SPORTY

Try mixing vintage and antique sports gear—aged leather boxing gloves can have a great patina—with luxe brass and sumptuous velvets. Vintage sports or physique photography can be elevated by a gilded frame and softened by a nearby bud vase. Stone and marble accents appeal to both more traditionally "masculine" and "feminine" aesthetics (don't get hung up on these old distinctions!), while candles, greenery, and similar accents have a neutral (but not boring) cachet.

2 RUSTIC + MODERN

Just because you have a penchant for the past doesn't mean your home has to be outfitted like an old-timey movie. Balance high tech and heirlooms by utilizing tech for utility—cord organizers, docking stations, and discreet cases for corralling techie bits and bobs will satisfy a gadget obsessive while maintaining a low profile that won't clash with a more retro sensibility. Mix inherited items, antiques, and farmhouse-inspired pieces in where appropriate.

They say opposites attract, right? Not necessarily when it comes to the design decisions inherent in merging your space with partners, kids, or roommates. It's easy to feel like they're invading this space you've worked so hard on. The secret is to find common interests, or pick up on unexpected and delightful points of harmony between your disparate inspirations.

3 GEN 7 KID + MIDCENTURY PARENT

Accommodating the toys, games, and other accouterments that tend to pile up can pose a real challenge to your sleek, refined design aesthetic. This means the right storage solutions are going to be key, and a good midcentury sideboard is a great place to start. Baskets and understated bins can be used for everything from building blocks to controllers and remotes, while some objects like vintage toys and stuffed animals could work on display—or even framed as art.

4 BEACH + URBAN

How can coastal charm and industrial chic coexist in harmony? Surprisingly well! Beach accents like driftwood and sea glass have a raw, organic quality that can complement industrial effects like brick and iron accents really nicely. Sandy hues and earth tones can bring warmth into a space dominated by cooler colors and materials like concrete and steel, while the right shade of ocean-evoking blue can create a cozy, soothing atmosphere that merges both aesthetics.

Cottage Industry

It's a fantasy shared by many city dwellers—the dream of leaving the concrete jungle behind for a creative experiment in a country idyll. But it's still relatively rare to find a young couple brave enough to take that ethos to heart. Nic Taylor and Jennifer Brandt-Taylor are one such couple.

While their New York City friends and neighbors assuaged the yen for nature with the odd rooftop garden, or weekend trips to the countryside, Taylor and Brandt-Taylor increasingly found that their bustling Murray Hill neighborhood proved more claustrophobic than conducive to good work.

"We needed peace and space," says Brandt-Taylor, an author and product designer who, with Taylor, makes up half the branding studio Thunderwing.

Six years ago, she and Taylor took the plunge, packing up home and business and heading for the sleepy Hudson Valley hamlet of Garrison, New York, swapping metropolitan mania for a quieter, more focused way of life. At first, their bucolic retreat was the very opposite of peaceful.

"It was terrifying," recalls Brandt-Taylor. "But living here has helped us creatively; [there's so much] natural beauty all around," she says.

The pair stumbled upon their new setting by happenstance. "We randomly walked into a real estate office [in Garrison]," recalls Brandt-Taylor,

"and they took us to an unlisted property by the water. We signed on the spot."

Taylor, who was born in nearby West Point, considers the move something of a homecoming—or, as he describes it, a "feeling of spiritual recirculation." The couple's house and headquarters, a two-story shingled cottage surrounded by lush, woodland-like landscaping at the end of a winding drive, was part of a complex of barns built in the 1920s.

Taylor readily admits that the couple initially found their new environment isolating. "For the first two years, our youngest friend was fifty-eight years old. But more people our age are moving here and starting families, bringing restaurants, cafés, yoga studios, and things we were starved for." It helps that they have established their own rituals and routines: for example, Brandt-Taylor cherishes "walking our pug around the property every evening to watch the sun set over the Hudson River and the Bear Mountain Bridge" as well as "Saturday-morning trips to the Cold Spring Farmers' Market on the grounds of the Boscobel Mansion."

The home is filled with choices that seemingly effortlessly merge the rustic setting with the thoroughly modern couple's interests. On one deep windowsill, an old turntable takes pride of place—a testament to Taylor's passion for collecting records, which is rivaled only by his wife's devotion to the written word. He points to the "versatility of technology and social media" as one of the biggest factors in pulling off a move like this. "You can really have it all—more living space, sweeping views, quiet nights with star-filled skies—while still feeling connected to your friends all over the world," he says. Welcome to the 21st-century version of frontier living.

We love how this couple's collected items are displayed— and actually put to use.

PREVIOUS SPREAD / SPACE TO RELAX

The couple spends most evenings unwinding in their comfortable, well-stocked library with their pug, Ali Baba, looking through books and talking about the day over a glass of wine.

OPPOSITE / WORK-LIFE BALANCE

An office workshop is attached by a covered walkway to the main building, allowing the two to work separately in tandem. "We text to make appointments with each other," says Brandt-Taylor with a laugh.

ABOVE LEFT / SHELF APPEAL

A rough-hewn shelving unit in the dining room hosts a collection of global tchotchkes and sentimental keepsakes, reflecting Taylor's passion for unique objects and memorabilia.

ABOVE RIGHT / TOOLS OF THE TRADE

In addition to the work he does for Thunderwing, Taylor still teaches graphic design and typography, and has a craftsman's appreciation for classic tools.

ABOVE / RESTING PLACE

The couple's bed is simply dressed in white linens. Underneath a fringed lampshade lies a stack of vintage magazines; a framed gallery poster is displayed above the makeshift headboard.

OPPOSITE / DOWN THE GARDEN PATH

Getting out of the city helped the couple to pay more attention to things that truly inspire them, such as the winding gravel paths lined with lush natural landscaping to create picturesque passageways through the grounds.

OPPOSITE / WORKING SPACE

Lined with original shelving, Taylor's studio space is rustic yet artful. Exposed weathered beams lend an unexpected elegance to the well-used and time-tested cabinets, flat files, and trays of lead type for the vintage letter press that inspired the couple to start Thunderwing.

RIGHT / VISUAL REFERENCE

Beside a series of books on Marilyn Monroe lies a print of the legendary screen siren. The couple also owns two collaged artworks by the legendary graphic designer Ivan Chermayeff, for whom Taylor interned after graduating from the School of Visual Arts in New York City.

This home combines rustic elements with really artful touches.

THE ART OF THE GALLERY WALL

A gallery wall can be integral to a home's look and feel-good design. Done right, it allows you to artfully blend seemingly disparate elements, pulling the whole space together. But how do you get it right? Where do you start? Read on for a few ideas that will help you determine what pieces work, how to arrange them and when and why to update everything to keep it fresh.

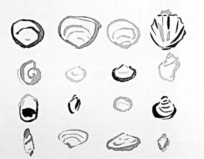

SCALE Play with proportion, mixing large and small elements and staggering heights of art or objects displayed on a shelf. Use a mix of frame styles—including no frame at all. There's really no right or wrong, just what appeals to your eye.

SPACING. Placing pieces with intention is key, so you'll want to lay everything out on the floor before drilling or nailing any holes in the walls. See if any themes emerge—your passion for a certain color, memories, or places—and group paintings and pieces by how similar they are (to play it safe) or switch it up and create an eclectic assemblage that feels true to you.

MIXING MEDIA AND COLOR

Consider framing an integral part of the gallery wall process, but don't get discouraged. If you can't afford custom framing, plan a way to work around that, whether it means you invest in some IKEA frames or simply create a cluster that sings sans framing. The paintings you have might similarly tell a very coherent color story or erupt in a riot of hues that aren't anywhere else in the room. Either approach is valid, the choice is all about your personal taste.

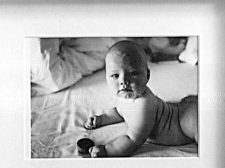

UPDATING IT OVER TIME. Working new pieces into an established arrangement can feel tricky. The key is to remember and reflect on why you placed certain pieces in the mix. Think about what elements of the arrangement make you happy, and what you feel might be missing—color, proportion, a portrait versus a landscape. This way you'll be ready to approach the remix with a plan.

Room to Grow

Jodie Patterson is no stranger to change and evolution. A social activist, author, and beauty entrepreneur, she was also a state champion gymnast and circus acrobat and is the mother of five. She writes and speaks on topics such as gender identity, entrepreneurship, family, and allyship.

Patterson has grown her design aesthetic through a number of spaces over the years, beginning with her childhood in a prewar building on New York's Riverside Drive. After graduating from Spelman College with a degree in literature, she lived in a raw, industrial loft and then in a classic brownstone, where she'd specified "every doorknob and fixture."

She found her new home in Brooklyn while going through a divorce, "I wanted a lot of space and I had all these requirements," she admits. Patterson and her ex-husband house-hunted together. A broker showed them what would become her new home and there was nothing specifically wow-ing about it, but it was large and convenient—new, very light, and big enough to accommodate Patterson's family *and* her furniture.

One of her favorite pieces is a sherbet-orange sofa in the living room, which she purchased at a flea market 18 years ago. Patterson has had the piece for years, and had taken it to an old tagging spot near PS1 where she and her daughter spray-painted it.

The only thing she didn't bring were light fixtures. "I love works in progress," Patterson says with a laugh, and lighting allows for relatively simple updates and changes. The lamps in the room right now are a pretty counterpoint to the heft of the seating; Patterson has

GORDON PARKS

made a ritual of turning each of them on at night.

Openness has been a recurring theme throughout Patterson's homes, not just as a design principle, but as a way of life. Whether she's in a classic brownstone or a modern loft, the pieces have always worked because they're personal. Flow-through floor plans create a sense of community and allow light to reach from front to back, while having multiple floors is "good for kids," notes Patterson, because they are allowed their own personal space while still being connected.

The family spends a lot of time in the open kitchen, where floor-to-ceiling windows, a crowd-friendly island

We love the idea of placing notes around your home—it really creates the space for brainstorming and growth.

and cozy benches create a relaxed atmosphere that invites lingering. "We can all fit in, in some configuration," Patterson says with a laugh. The top two floors of the home are in use all the time, with communal spaces on the main floor, bedrooms upstairs, and the "kid's area" downstairs. A hallway upstairs functions as a reading nook, a respite from the madding crowds below.

Patterson's mementos and decorative keepsakes tend to have stories behind them. She displays heirlooms and old photos on the walls, gallery-style, so that her past is always present, saying "I use them to remind me, visually, of what's important. They do nothing for me in a photo album."

PREVIOUS SPREAD /
ROOM FOR ALL
Patterson's favorite furnishings have moved with her over the years. "The pieces I purchase aren't expensive, but maintaining them has been," she says.

OPPOSITE / PRETTY IN PINK
Patterson has focused intently on fabrics and finding ones that last. She declares the twin lounge chairs in hot pink "the personality of the room."

ABOVE / FAMILY TIME
The home's open interior supports family togetherness. In the warmer months, the family can use the expansive back patio to shoot hoops or chill out.

OPPOSITE / LET IT SHINE

"Even when I was in the brownstone, I made it feel more like a loft," says Patterson of her preference for open, airy spaces, flooded with light.

ABOVE / PERSONALITY PLUS

Although she's lived in seventeen homes in twenty-five years, Patterson has never once hired a decorator to interpret her personal style.

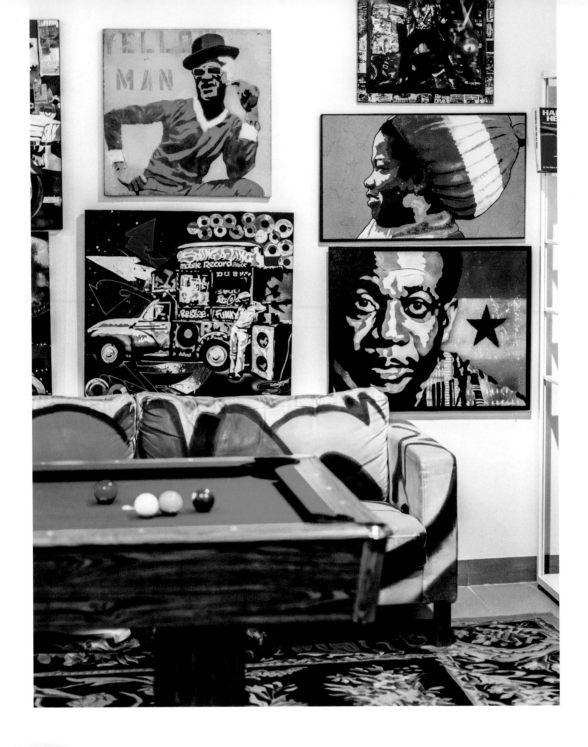

Creating an artistic moment with color and interesting items is always a good design choice.

ABOVE / KID STUFF
The top two floors of the home are in use all the time, with communal spaces on the main floor, bedrooms upstairs, and a dedicated "kid's area" downstairs featuring a drum set and pool table.

OPPOSITE / WALL-TO-WALL STYLE
Patterson's vibrant personality is on display throughout the home, with a mix of family photos and colorful, eye-catching art. Every piece has a story.

Four Ways to Add Life with Plants

1 CREATE HEIGHT

Use taller plants strategically to draw the eye upwards or along a blank wall. Plants can also be used to create rooms within a room, such as dividing up a large space in an open floor plan—think of a potted palm or tall fronds demarcating a living room from a dining area. Hanging planters, hung solo or in groups at varying heights, can create a dynamic visual composition.

2 ADD VISUAL INTEREST AND TEXTURE

Air plants and succulents are low maintenance and affordable—plus they're cute to look at! Try incorporating a single cactus or intriguing air plant into an unexpected corner for some visual texture and cheer, or, if minimalism isn't your thing, populate an entire windowsill with different varieties. They're a great way to bring an organic, graphic element into a space that's otherwise sleek and streamlined.

There's nothing quite like plants to make your space come to life—literally. Bringing living decor into your home encourages mindfulness and healthy living. Beyond that, being surrounded by things you love can encourage personal expression as well as creativity, change and growth. Here are some ways to incorporate plants into your home life.

3 USE PLANTS AS ART

If the very idea of keeping plants alive makes you nervous, look to arrangements and accents that never need watering. Dried blooms can be displayed in a vessel or dish as potpourri, or even framed; sticks and other bits of foliage can also be incorporated into different floral tableaux to create a little shrine to the outdoors. Exotic leaves can be painted or even decoupaged for a graphic element.

4 DELIGHT THE SENSES

Plants are more than just a visual delight; they can also provide a feast for the olfactory senses. Fresh blooming flowers such as lush lilies or exotic orchids perfume the air, while dried rose petals and lavender can create breathable moments of bliss and serve as a reminder to unwind. In the kitchen, fresh herbs grown in pots or a sunny window box can liven up your day *and* your dinner.

A Big Move

Dabito is a lifestyle blogger, photographer, artist, décor guru, tastemaker, passionate vintage hunter, and lover of all things design. He and his partner, Ryan Bennett, had never cohabited before moving in together and, in fact, the couple had just met months before they decided to take the plunge on buying a home together.

They established themselves near Ryan's job as a middle school principal in New Orleans, Louisiana. It was a big move for Dabito, who had lived previously in New York and Los Angeles. Still, he recalls, when they found the house together online after just four months of dating, "we fell in love with it, and then we got it."

Both Dabito and Bennett are first-time homeowners, which presented its own set of tribulations, including heavy rains and a leaky roof

that threatened their attic.

But the couple acclimated to the challenges of home ownership well. Their styles are compatible, says Dabito, even though their first big fight was indeed about decorating. "Ryan was so nervous about me purging all of his things," remembers Dabito. They have since successfully merged their thankfully similar styles, but when it comes down to it, "if I want something, I'm going to get it regardless!" says Dabito.

The 2,100-square-foot home has three bedrooms and a

While this home features a lot of color and pattern, it also feels organized and calming.

sizable outdoor area for entertaining. Having lived most recently in a New York City apartment, Dabito was initially overwhelmed at the prospect of outfitting an entire home in his signature style.

"I think small spaces are easier in a lot of ways," he says. "It took a couple of years to really get it right."

As for the compromises they've made, Dabito says, "There are challenges that come up living with anyone. "Even some of the brass elements I wanted to use throughout—Ryan thought they were too gaudy. But then, one day, he bought me brass flatware for my birthday. It just takes time!"

PREVIOUS SPREAD / WIDE OPEN SPACE

The vintage striped sofa in the parlor room is from
Chairish and was initially a point of contention for
the couple. But now, Bennett loves it.

OPPOSITE / SETTLING IN

The sunroom became a multipurpose living area, and
Bennett took the design reins, painting one exterior
wall black and custom-designing an addition in the
form of a pergola to increase the home's usable
square footage year-round.

ABOVE LEFT / MIX AND MATCH

"No matter how many gallery walls you've probably
seen over the years," Dabito says, "it will never
go out of style. It's such a great way to add visual
interest to an otherwise blank space."

ABOVE RIGHT / SWEET DREAMS

"Our bedroom always felt a bit blah to us," Dabito
says. Adding this lush, green wallpaper accent wall
made all the difference.

ABOVE / LATIN ACCENTS

On a recent visit to Peru, Dabito says he went a little crazy over all their gorgeous textiles, adding "Clearly, I didn't buy enough. I wanna go back so badly!"

OPPOSITE / WORKING SPACE

The couple entertains frequently, hosting Ryan's school functions in their large, open-plan parlor room, in one corner of which Dabito carved out a work nook.

ABOVE LEFT / FRESHEN UP
The couple replaced old tiling and flooring in the master bathroom
and added a standing shower to keep things fresh and modern.

ABOVE RIGHT / IN THE CORNER
Dabito turned to second-hand shopping on eBay and Chairish to find
many of the colorful and eclectic furnishing and accessories throughout the home.

ABOVE LEFT / WORLD OF WONDERS

The couple's shared love of travel is expressed in Peruvian textiles, Moroccan rugs, bountiful basketry, and a host of worldly souvenirs woven throughout each room.

ABOVE RIGHT / UPWARD TREND

After a trip to South Africa, Dabito developed a fascination with baskets, arranging them in loosely grouped upward flights of color and texture.

Never be afraid to make your space as creative as you are.

Credits & Acknowledgements

FRONT OF BOOK p. 2 Photographed by Philip Ficks, styled by Kate Jordan. p. 8 Photographed by Nicole LaMotte. p. 10 Photographed by Mikola Accuardi, styled by Mikhael Roman. pp. 12–13 Photographed by Julia Robbs, styled by Katja Greeff.

CHAPTER 1 p. 16 *Left* photographed by Jessie Webster, styled by Rebecca Buenik; *right* photographed by Ana Kamin. p. 17 *left* photographed by Amy Bartlam; *right* photographed by Ana Kamin. p. 19 Photographed by Erin Kunkel. p. 20 Photographed by Nicole LaMotte. pp. 22–29 Photographed by Amy Bartlam. pp. 30-31 Photographed by Naomi McColloch, styled by Bryson Gill. Stained glass courtesy of General Store. pp. 32–39 Photographed by Nicole Franzen, styled by Katja Greeff. p. 40 Photographed by Naomi McColloch, styled by Bryson Gill. pp. 42–49 Photographed by Genevieve Garruppo. Styled by Sarah Jean Shelton. p. 50 Photographed by Dawn Heumann. p. 51 Photographed by Nicki Sebastian. pp. 52–59 Photographed by Philip Ficks, styled by Kate Jordan. pp. 60–61 Photographed by Naomi McColloc, styled by Bryson Gill. Essence bottle courtesy of Hudson Grace. pp. 62–69 Photographed by Claudia Uribe Touri.

CHAPTER 2 p. 72 *Top* photographed by Nicole LaMotte; *bottom* photographed by Mikola Accuardi, styled by Mikhael Roman. p. 73 *Top* photographed by Virginia Rollison; *bottom* photographed by Nicole LaMotte. p. 75 Photographed by Nicole LaMotte. p. 76 Photographed by Nicole Franzen, styled by Katja Greeff. pp. 78–85 Photographed by Erin Kunkel. p. 86 Photographed by Amy Plumb. p. 87 Photographed by Andrea Posadas. pp. 88–95 Photographed by Jenna Peffley, styled by Tammy Price/Fragments Identity. pp. 96–97 Photographed by Naomi McColloch, styled by Bryson Gill. pp. 98–105 Photographed by Julia Robbs, styled by Katja Greeff. pp. 106–107 Photographed by Naomi McColloch, styled by Bryson Gill. pp. 108–115 Photographed by Ana Kamin. pp. 116–117 Photographed by Naomi McColloch, styled by Bryson Gill. Thanks to Corie Altaffer and Molly O'Neil Stewart for assistance in decorating chairs. pp. 118–125 Photographed by Gaelle LeBoulicaut.

CHAPTER 3 p. 128 *Top* photographed by Nicole LaMotte; *bottom* by Sabrina Bot. p. 129 *Top* photographed by Jessie Webster, styled by Rebecca Buenik; *bottom* photographed by Maria del Rio, styled by Field Theory/Leah Harmatz. p. 131 Photographed by Jenna Peffley, styled by Tammy Price/Fragments Identity. p. 132 Photographed by Genevieve Garruppo, styled by Sarah Jean Shelton. pp. 134–141 Photographed by Anna-Alexia Basile. p. 142 Photographed by Michael Wiltbank. p. 143 Photographed by Kelsey Wilson. pp. 144–151 Photographed by Anna Powell Teeter. pp. 152–153 Photographed by Naomi McColloch, styled by Bryson Gill. pp. 154–161 Photographed by Ashley Batz. pp. 162–163 Photographed by Naomi McColloch, styled by Bryson Gill. Thanks to Angela Tofoya for providing the pink bowl, candle, pillow, and wallpaper. pp. 164–171 Photographed by Sean Litchfield, styled by Kaylei McGaw. pp. 172–173 Photographed by Naomi McColloch, styled by Bryson Gill. pp. 174–181 Photographed by Hilton Carter.

CHAPTER 4 p. 184 *Top* photographed by Maria del Rio, styled by Field Theory/Leah Harmatz; *bottom* photographed by Mikola Accuardi, styled by Mikhael Roman. p. 185 *Top* photographed by Ruth Maria Murphy; *bottom* photographed by Maria del Rio, styled by Field Theory/Leah Harmatz. p. 187 Photographed by Genevieve Garruppo. p. 188 Photographed by Omi Tanaka. 190-197 Photographed by Genevieve Garruppo, styled by Sarah Jean Shelton. p. 198 Photographed by Mike Vorrasi. p. 199 Photographed by Erin Yamagata. pp. 200–207 Photographed by Becky Kimball. pp. 208–209 Photographed by Naomi McColloch, styled by Bryson Gill. Thanks to Cleveland & Kennedy for the pillows. pp. 210–217 Photographed by Genevieve Garruppo. pp. 218–219 Photographed by Naomi McColloch, styled by Bryson Gill. Thanks to Hudson Grace for the crystal votive and scandi wooden board. pp. 220–227 Photographed by Michael Wells. pp. 228–229 Photographed by Naomi McColloch, styled by Bryson Gill. 230-237 Photographed by Jessie Webster, styled by Rebecca Buenik.

CHAPTER 5 p. 240 *Left* Photographed by Nana Hagel; *right* Photographed by Jenna Peffley. Styled by Tammy Price/Fragments Identity. p. 241 Photographed by Virginia Rollison p. 243 Photographed by Jenna Peffley, Styled by Tammy Price/Fragments Identity. p. 244 Photographed by Randy Schmidt. p. 246 Photographed by Syed Aqeen Photography. p. 247 Photographed by Anna-Alexia Basile. p. 248-255 Photographed by Tessa Neustadt. pp. 256–257 Photographed by Naomi McColloch, styled by Bryson Gill. Basket vase with driftwood courtesy of Dear Keaton. pp. 258–265 Photographed by Genevieve Garruppo. pp. 266–267 Photographed by Naomi McColloch, styled by Bryson Gill. Large framed painting courtesy of Jenny Pennywood. pp. 268–275 Photographed by Omi Tanaka. pp. 276–277 Photographed by Naomi McColloch, syled by Bryson Gill. pp. 278–285 Photographed by Randy Schmidt.

FINAL IMAGE Photographed by Jessica Sample

WELDON OWEN WOULD LIKE TO THANK: Kelly Scanlon Design for advice on fixtures; Jenny Pennywood for spine swatches; Lisa Marietta for editorial expertise, Tamara White for photo retouching.

About the Author

Sean Santiago is a Brooklyn-based lifestyle writer, photographer, and design influencer. An advocate for linens and greige, his work has been featured in outlets as varied as *Vogue, Architectural Digest, Sight Unseen,* and *PIN-UP*. As Senior Associate Editor at Lonny he contributed to a multitude of pieces, from hands-on DIY projects to extensive celebrity home tours to European travel tips.

About Lonny

Lonny is here to make home design and decor feel accessible and approachable for everyone. Founded in 2009, *Lonny* was an early pioneer in the digital shelter space, and it continues to be the go-to digital resource for millions of readers and tastemakers seeking inspiration and resources for making their homes more beautiful. *Lonny* believes that personal style and creativity are the building blocks of a happy space – because everyone deserves a home that brings them joy.

Lonny would like to thank Briana Gagnier, Shelby Wax, Megan O'Sullivan, Erica Carter, Kelly Booth, and Molly Stewart.

Sean Santiago, who took our seed of an outline and made it explode with personality and expertise.

Everyone on the Weldon Owen team, including Mariah Bear and Lucie Parker, who devoted their energy to making this book happen.

The original founders of *Lonny,* Patrick Cline and Michelle Adams, as well as everyone who has dedicated their creativity to making *Lonny* the brand it is today.

Everyone who opened up their home or lent us their voice or point of view for this book, a big thank you to you, as well.

And, of course, YOU for being a dedicated and loyal *Lonny* reader – we hope you love this book as much as we do.

weldon**owen**

President & Publisher *Roger Shaw*
SVP Sales & Marketing *Amy Kaneko*
Associate Publisher *Mariah Bear*
Senior Editor *Lucie Parker*
Editor *Molly O'Neill Stewart*
Associate Editor *Ian Cannon*
Creative Director *Kelly Booth*
Art Director *Lorraine Rath*
Freelance Art Director *Jennifer Durrant*
Production Designers *Howie Severson, Lou Bustsmante, and Lisa Berman*
Production Director *Michelle Duggan*
Imaging Manager *Don Hill*

Lonny Lessons & Art of Images

Photographer *Naomi McColloch*
Stylist *Bryson Gill*
Digital Tech *Andrew Williams*
Stylist's Assistant *Kyle Emory Peck*

© 2019 Weldon Owen International
1045 Sansome Street, Suite 100
San Francisco, CA 94111
www.weldonowen.com

ISBN 978-168188-324-3
10 9 8 7 6 5 4 3 2 1
2019 2020 2021 2022
Printed in China